Muti

Mutiny

How Our World is Tilting

PETER MERTENS

First published in April 2024

LeftWord Books
2254/2A Shadi Khampur
New Ranjit Nagar
New Delhi 110008
INDIA

LeftWord Books and Vaam Prakashan are imprints of
Naya Rasta Publishers Pvt. Ltd.

leftword.com

ISBN   978-93-92018-63-3 (paperback)
          978-93-92018-77-0 (e-book)

Printed and bound by Chaman Enterprises, New Delhi

Contents

Chapter 4: Mutiny

Chapter 5: Missed Opportunities

Chapter 6: The Voices Below Deck

Acknowledgements

For dearest Nadine, simply for being there, as a sounding board and anchor; for my mother, her understanding glance and unconditional support; for Gille Feyaerts, partner in crime, tower of strength, always uplifting me in the difficult moments; for Hugo Franssen, the patient word magician who brings every text to life; for Thomas Blommaert, supporter and publisher of the best book team of the Low Countries; for Mario Debaene, for the fresh cover design of this book; for Ben Van Duppen, along with David Pestieau, the heart and soul of our research centre; for Wim and Christophe, André and Marc, Mathieu and Olivier, for their contributions; for Bert, Benjamin, Kim, David, Ann, Koen and Johan, for proofreading the first draft; for Annik, Tim, Koen and Kenneth, and the summer evening on our terrace; for Loes, Christophoros, Jenny, Kevin, Adrien, Benjamin, Charlotte, Michael and their remarkable docuseries; for Liselotte, Tom and Brecht, who have turned the book into an entertaining podcast; for Ivo, who always lends a helping hand; for my comrades in the party executive, who shouldered all my duties; and for Erwin, Elisabeth, and all the patient translators. *Gracias!*

Foreword

Surplus Profits, Surplus Humanity

VIJAY PRASHAD

You don't need to be a statistician or an economist to be able to read the basic facts in the world today: the dominant classes and the corporations that they control extract surplus profits from the wealth produced by society, while billions of human beings who work to produce that wealth find themselves treated as if they are surplus humanity. This immense social divide, a widening gap across the class structure, can be observed in almost every single country in the world. This gap is not the result of any natural development, let alone of that magical phrase 'the Market'. This chasm across human society is produced and reproduced solely because of a civilizational system that privileges the private property of the few above the social needs of the many. That system is known as capitalism, a dynamic social process that – through inter-capitalist competition, through advancements in science and technology, and through better utilisation of the ingenuity of humans – has led to vast increases in productivity but at the same

9

time – because of private property – to immense social inequality. This double movement of capitalism, which generates enormous social wealth and enormous social inequality, both confounds humanity and provides immense potential for solutions to our great dilemmas – solutions that we call socialism.

The social and political consequences of this chasm are not as easy to define as the chasm itself. For the past hundred years, social scientists have studied the increase in desolation despite the vast modern advances in society. Atomisation, alienation, depression, anxiety – disorders of the mind and body have come to shape so much of the landscape of human emotions. These feelings are not ahistorical, rooted deep in the psyche to torment human beings outside the social conditions of our lives. Fields of sociology and psychology root these traumas in this social schizophrenia – vast wealth and vast inequality, the socialisation of labour, and the atomisation of human interactions. Salves can be applied, but these will not ultimately solve the underlying problem.

Within this social situation, people understand their predicament in very different ways, which is what provides the ground for political disputes. Some people recognise the class realities and join unions of follow workers and political parties of the left, working hard to build their confidence, clarity, and power as we confront the tough granite block of power. Others, seeing the same reality, come to believe that their only salvation is in personal advancement – perhaps in becoming an entrepreneur or in getting lucky in the great casino of modern capitalism, the financial markets. And yet others, disappointed with reality, turn against their fellow workers who are different from them and who are socially marginalised (such as migrants). The 'surplus population', unable to get its hands on the 'surplus profits' that could address our human needs, either lifts the red flag and marches down the street, goes inward, or turns on each other. From the standpoint of the left, the first option – the red flag – is preferred, but it is not an automatic decision.

Peter Mertens' book – *Mutiny* – goes into the heart of this predicament. Mertens, the General Secretary of the Workers' Party of Belgium (PTB-PVDA), documents both the surplus profits of the mega-corporations (particularly those that produce energy and food) and the conditions of surplus humanity, humanity that capitalism uses but does not acknowledge. It goes to the heart of the Marxist tradition for movement intellectuals to go amongst the people as they struggle to survive and to build another system, document their ideas and their emotions, and then theorise this knowledge to build a systematic understanding of the current conjuncture to better know how to act in the world. Mertens' *Mutiny* is in line with that tradition, a book that builds its theory from the facts, and it takes its facts from the experiences of workers in struggle across the world, from Indian farmers to British nurses.

Class realities, however transparent they might appear, do not always define the battlelines of struggle. Layers of social experience obscure the clarities of class struggle, including geopolitical shifts, the neo-colonial structures, and aspirations of groups that struggle against wretched social hierarchies. As the chasm in the class system widens, other gaps emerge, such as between the rising powers of the world (Brazil, China, India, Indonesia, Mexico, South Africa, and others) and the neo-colonial powers (the countries in the North Atlantic Treaty Organisation – NATO, for instance). A realisation has set in across the North Atlantic that the re-emergence of China threatens the neo-colonial structure and the seemingly permanent power of the NATO countries. Despite the vast resources to settle the problems of environmental and climate devastation and social inequality, the richer countries of NATO prefer to go to war to defend their petty privileges (including the genocidal war against the Palestinians, with apartheid Israel's particular focus on Gaza). They prefer to squander trillions of dollars a year on military waste rather than fund energy transitions or to end hunger. For the starving people in the world, clarities have begun to emerge – NATO's military spending is far less attractive than the Chinese socialist project to eradicate absolute poverty. To counter this clarity, the NATO states now pursue a reckless New Cold War on China at the same time as they refuse to allow any reasonable negotiation with Russia in a futile war in Ukraine. This is the class struggle on a global scale. When most European politicians, including many on the left, either remain silent on the obscenities of imperialism or fall prey to the warmongering, Mertens stands firm, adopts a global perspective against Eurocentrism and jingoism, and recognises that the complexities of the moment – not the purities of ideology – define the line of march for the working-class globally, including inside Europe.

There are now a billion mutinies across the planet. The mood of this mutiny comes to us at different scales: mutinies in workplaces, mutinies in societies, and mutinies of countries. These mutinies are not all decipherable through the same logic; many of them – such as the coups in Africa's Sahel – require detailed assessments built on their own political possibilities. It would be naïve to imagine that these mutinies can simply be arithmetically added up into a unity. It will take considerable work to unite these mutinies, unify people, and build the world we need to build if humanity and the planet are to survive.

Santiago, Chile
January 2024

Introduction

Palestine, a Tipping Point

It is 11 November 2023, the day on which the guns fall silent. Except the guns are not silent. In recent weeks, more kilotons of bombs have been dropped on Gaza than on Hiroshima and Nagasaki in 1945.

Nadia is a Palestinian. She lives and works in Ghent. She shows me photos of the fifteen family members she has lost in the past month. Nephews, nieces, uncles, brothers, and sisters. Fifteen people no longer with us; fifteen out of (at that time) ten thousand dead. I'm speechless.

We are entering a new phase of this unrestrained and merciless violence being broadcast live on television. Evidently, international law and universal human rights can only exist if they are consistently invoked, even against the world's mightiest and greatest aggressors.

In this book, I talk about five watershed moments between the Global North and the Global South in recent years. 'Is this a sixth tipping point?', people ask me. It most certainly is. The war against Palestine rips off the emperor's clothes. The axis of war fuelled by Washington is resorting to extreme violence, but it is more isolated than ever. The double standards and hypocrisy are being exposed all over the world.

From Jakarta to Brussels, London to Johannesburg, Istanbul

to Washington, a new generation is standing up for Palestine. Millions are taking to the streets for peace, bread, and justice. This offers a key perspective. I hope this book can serve as a framework for all those raising their voices against injustice, both in the Global North and Global South.

Antwerp (Belgium)
November 2023

Chapter 1

The Summer of Discontent

Kath

I'm talkin' mutiny
I said I'm takin' over
U gotta give up the ship
U gotta take a little trip
    The Family, *Mutiny*

At four every afternoon, the seventh Duchess of Bedford feels peckish. And it makes her moody. She doesn't really fancy waiting for dinner. Fortunately, her servants find a way to defuse the situation: the noblewoman is served a light meal with a cup of tea. Ever since the Duchess of Bedford had her way, tea has been drunk with a biscuit in the afternoon across England. True or not, this is the legend of high tea.

It's four o'clock in the afternoon. Kath already made the tea in her floral cup this morning. 'It's the electricity bill, you know. I boil a kettle in the mornings now. The rest goes into my flask. Every penny counts'. Kath is bent over the flowerpots in her small plant garden. 'My plants are my therapy. They relax me after my shift. I can put the day's work behind me', she says, planting seeds with care in a flower bed. Her morning shift at the hospital is over. 'I earn exactly what I did ten years ago; only life has become much more expensive. In fact, my salary has gone down by a fifth. Many nurses try to earn a little extra now with a second job'.

The hospital corridors are buzzing with stories. People do an extra two or three hours to make the day worthwhile. Colleagues wear two pullovers at home in the winter to save on heating costs. One nurse had to cancel her daughter's piano lessons. Some people walk to work to save on the expense of public transport. Others even call in sick at the end of the month because they can't afford the transport to work.

'I've been a nurse for thirty years. In all that time, it has never occurred to me to go on strike. It's just not in my nature'. Kath tries to hide what she's feeling as she tells the story. 'We've talked about it so much at work. I'm worried about the future of the NHS (National Health Service) and the young people entering the profession. I've seen so many of them leave. They get jobs elsewhere, in a supermarket or something. Because they just can't cope with healthcare any longer. If we don't make our voices heard now, it will all be ruined'.

It's tough for her, but Kath has decided to take action.

~ ~ ~

'COVID hit us hard. But when the pandemic passed, and the applause faded, the government forgot all about the healthcare sector. It happened very quickly. And it's so wrong, so very wrong'. Pat Cullen's tone is serious. She has been a nurse for close to forty years. Nursing is in her blood, she says. She is the youngest of six girls, four of whom went into nursing. In 2021, she became the leader of the Royal College of Nursing, the RCN, a nurses' union with almost half a million members. There is something cautious and composed about Pat Cullen.

It's not easy to strike in the United Kingdom. By law, trade unions must consult their members every six months to check their willingness to act. If the majority agrees, the union can only issue a strike notice during the following six months.

Pat Cullen spent months attempting to negotiate with the health minister over the low pay in the healthcare sector. But the minister would not entertain the subject. By an overwhelming majority, up to 90 per cent, half a million nurses in the hospitals of

England, Northern Ireland, and Wales voted to strike.

The RCN finally issued a strike notice for 15 December 2022, ten days before Christmas. The union is determined to negotiate a real pay increase: 5 per cent above the rate of inflation. And it is calling for more investment in the public healthcare sector. 'I believe most viewers realise that the nurses' wage demands are unreasonable', claims a straight-faced prime minister, Rishi Sunak, on national television.

What is reasonable is a matter of perspective. People who can't make ends meet despite their hard work and dedication see things differently than someone having a heated luxury pool built with a £250,000 price tag in the garden of their listed mansion during an energy crisis, which is what Prime Minister Rishi Sunak is doing. His private pool uses so much energy that the local power grid must be strengthened to meet the demand for electricity. It gives an altogether different picture of worldly concerns.

The RCN makes a last-ditch attempt to reach an agreement. But Pat Cullen sighs dejectedly as she leaves the cabinet building: 'It wasn't a good meeting. You know, when a minister comes into the room with five men. They say they're shocked to hear that a nurse could be the family's primary breadwinner. These gentlemen think that being a nurse is some kind of second income on which a family cannot depend. They have no idea'. The implication is that it doesn't really matter that nurses are underpaid. It is 2023, and some conservatives still can't get their heads around the idea of a female breadwinner.

And so the inevitable happens. Half a million nurses go on strike for the first time in the RCN's 100-plus-year history. When Kath reaches the picket line at the Royal Berkshire Hospital, hundreds of nurses are already waiting, wrapped up in their big winter coats. Drivers honk their horns in support. 'Never thought I'd ever be out here', a nurse tells her. 'I'm getting all weepy'. She gets a warm hug from her colleagues.

~~~

Six months later, I took the train to London. On my arrival at St. Pancras International, a friendly pamphleteer thrusts a flyer into my hand: *Peaky Blinders: The Immersive Experience.* An inside look at Netflix's fictional Shelby family, masters of crime in post-WWI England. The series is set in Birmingham, but some filming was done in London. 'Explore sets, complete challenges, and interact with iconic characters from the show with this ticket to the immersive experience at The Camden Garrison'. No matter how hard the flyer tries, I have to pass this up because I have an appointment with the economist Grace Blakeley. Rather than the economic crime scene of the inter-war period, she investigates the current economy.

'There are criminal sides to that, too', she laughs jovially. With her books, publications, and interviews, Blakeley, who has just turned thirty, has already made a name for herself. In today's London, the red brick factory walls of the Peaky Blinders sets have been replaced by glass financial towers. Probably a sign of the times. 'It was changed to remove workers from the scene and place the bankers and billionaires centre stage', she tells me. 'We were told that employees no longer matter. Class no longer mattered. It was just a matter of moving ones and zeros – all about the money being shifted around. And maybe, we were told, some wealth would trickle down to us. But that, of course, never happened'.

During the darkest days of the pandemic, it became abundantly clear who was running the show. Working excessively long hours for low wages and rapidly eroding working conditions, yet still pulling the chestnuts out of the fire in the thick of the COVID-19 storm, a certain consciousness emerged, a budding class consciousness. Applause is no longer enough to silence that class. It's cash down or no go, especially with food prices going through the roof.

For many status-quo politicians, social class is outmoded. In their view, income from labour or income from capital doesn't make much difference these days. For them, class divisions are a relic of the time when Charles Dickens authored his novels – like stale bread.

Nothing could be further from the truth, argues Grace Blakeley. 'The world is run in the interests of the powerful. But it doesn't have to be that way. Because workers produce things, the real things, the things we need for survival. While the people at the top are juggling spreadsheets, the working class is out there, making the products you see on the shelves every day'.

The pandemic and the cost-of-living crisis have brought back the concept of *social class*. Those who live off their labour are in a different social category to those who live off capital. Your class determines where you work, where and how you live, and what you eat. Your class affects your health, your children's education, and often your chances in court. *Class matters*.

As of August 2023, as I complete this book, UK workers have endured 20 consecutive months of impoverishment. Throughout this entire period, inflation has exceeded the meagre wage increases. It has been a huge income shock.

At the other end of the spectrum, the reverse is happening. The profits of the 350 largest listed companies in the UK have soared by 73 per cent over the past three years. As shareholders are the primary beneficiaries of this vein of gold, the ranks of multimillionaires are growing. And the four richest Britons now own more combined than the 20 million poorest.

'I know many of us are embarrassed if we go to a food bank. But you shouldn't be. You have to support your family. This is precisely why we are campaigning for decent wages', says a bus driver. The spin doctors who try to erase class differences are usually clueless about the real situation of large sections of the working class.

Injustice is the breeding ground of all resistance, even today. Even though the UK is experiencing the biggest wave of strikes in decades, the media barely covers it. One summer of discontent has rolled via an even bigger winter of discontent into another hot summer of disputes.

Millions are laying down their tools as the strikes spread throughout society. Nurses, doctors, teachers, civil servants, dockworkers, lecturers, firefighters, paramedics, bus drivers, postal workers, baggage handlers, rail workers, and a host of others are involved. So many walkouts are happening in so many sectors that the BBC has to keep a calendar of who is working where and when across the country.

'The working class is back, and we refuse to be poor anymore'. Mick Lynch's words reverberate around the packed room of The Clapham Grand in Battersea, London. It's another union rally in the Enough is Enough campaign focused on rising living costs and stagnant wages. Mick Lynch is the general secretary of the National Union of Rail, Maritime and Transport Workers (RMT), one of the driving forces behind the long summer of discontent. He makes his voice heard, loud and clear:

> 'People are fed up with the way they've been treated. The British worker is basically underpaid and gets no dignity or respect in the workplace. Enough is enough. It's time to act in our class interests. If we fight together, we are an unstoppable force in this society!'[1]

~ ~ ~

Precisely 255 years ago, in 1768, sailors in Sunderland decided to 'strike the sails' to voice their grievances and demands for better working conditions. Considered a 'mutiny' at the time, it was one of the first major work stoppages. Ever since that mutiny that saw sailors 'striking the sails', the word strike has become the

1 Sophia Sleigh, 'The Working Class Is Back and We Refuse To Be Poor Anymore – Mick Lynch Tells Crowd', *Huffington Post*, 18 August 2022.

established term for a work stoppage.[2] The on-land mutiny for better working conditions quickly spread throughout fledgling industrial England.

The social struggle has been ebbing and flowing like the tide ever since. But it is there, open and active, or slumbering and waiting for the sails to be struck. In France, a full-scale pension revolt has been sweeping the country for months. In Germany and the Netherlands, strikes have suddenly flared up in sectors that seemed to have been dormant for years. Meanwhile, here in Belgium, there is fierce and persistent opposition to retail chain Delhaize's franchising and wage dumping. The great summer of discontent, which has been dragging on in the UK for more than a year, revolves mostly around wages and prices.

2 Niklas Frykman, Clare Anderson, Lex Heerma van Voss and Marcus Rediker, 'Mutiny and Maritime Radicalism in the Age of Revolution: An Introduction', *International Review of Social History*, Volume 58, Special Issue S21: *Mutiny and Maritime Radicalism in the Age of Revolution: A Global Survey*, 2013, pp.1-14.

Food

Talking about food is
frowned upon in higher circles.
The reason being, they've
already eaten.
  Bertolt Brecht

In early August 2023, casually buried somewhere in the back of newspapers is the following: 'More than one in ten people in Germany cannot afford a nutritious meal at least once a day'. This is based on information from Eurostat, the European Commission's statistical agency.

People read what they want, but I read this again. In Germany, one of the world's richest economies, 11.4 per cent of the population cannot afford a meal with meat, poultry or fish, or an equivalent vegetarian alternative, at least every other day. That's more than ten million people. Single parents suffer the most. At least every other day, nearly one in five of them – 19.3 per cent to be exact – forgoes a proper nutritious meal. The same is true for their children.[1] High food prices are becoming a determining factor in how more and more people eat.

The list I read out in the plenary session of Parliament is still vivid in my memory: 'Eggs up 31 per cent; full-fat milk up 35 per cent; potatoes up 27 per cent; sugar up 32 per cent'. It was a plea for a temporary price freeze on a basket of basic foodstuffs and a proposal quickly brushed off by the majority parties.

Real food spending in Germany, Italy, and France is now

---

1 Ralf Wurzbacher, 'Folgen der Inflation. Essen als Luxus', *junge Welt*, 1 August 2023, p.5.

around 6-7 per cent lower than before the pandemic.[2] Not restaurant visits, but weekly consumption of milk, meat, fish, eggs, fruits, and vegetables. This is partly what stoked the flames of the British summer of discontent. As Kate Bell, former chief economist (and now assistant general secretary) of the Trades Union Congress, pointed out: 'One in seven workers are having to skip meals.'[3]

'Unfortunately, the days of seeing food prices fall, that does seem to be something that we may not be seeing for a little while yet, if in the future at all.' Huw Pill, the Bank of England's chief economist, said this with a heavy sigh to the public broadcaster, the BBC. While food prices may drop slightly, Pill is adamant that a time of cheap food is not on the horizon. That's where climate change fits in.[4]

In some circles, it's the done thing to get tough on climate change. But we've been down this road before, haven't we? No, not yet. Today's temperatures are the highest they have ever been since the emergence of cities and agriculture in the fertile deltas of the Tigris and Euphrates, the Indus and Yangtze, and the rivers of Peru about ten thousand years ago. But how do we know that, you might ask? From the layers: researchers are drilling into the ice cores and examining the different layers of ice. From all the information released, the World Meteorological Organization deduces that the Earth has not been as hot in 120,000 years. July 2023 was the hottest month ever recorded on the planet. 'It's entirely usual for food prices to fluctuate alongside the seasons, but the exceptionally hot and dry summer being experienced from Europe to the US, to Asia and beyond has caused poor harvests and many crops to fail', the World Economic Forum reports. 'The climate crisis is making

2 Joseph Politano, 'The EU's Fragile Recovery', *Apricitas Economics*, 9 August 2023.

3 Simon Bellens, 'Britse vakbonden en de strijd tegen het spook van Thatcher', *Visie*, 24 December 2022.

4 'Higher food prices may be here to stay, says Bank economist', *BBC.com*, 7 August 2023.

extreme weather – from heatwaves and droughts to storms and floods – more common, and some crops are more susceptible to these changes than others'.[5]

Much of the Mediterranean region is experiencing extreme drought, damaging many olive trees and causing the olive harvest to fail. Rice production in Italy is also threatened, as it is in California's major rice-growing region. In India, exceptionally heavy monsoon rains have washed away rice crops, and the country has halted exports of both white and broken rice. Over the past four months, rice prices in Asia have risen by 15 per cent.

After years of severe drought, many regions of Argentina have declared a state of emergency, with the production of wheat, soybeans and corn heavily disrupted. Soy is used for animal feed. An increase in the price of soy immediately affects the price and availability of meat and dairy products.

We could continue to list essential products affected by the climate crisis. To summarise, global food prices have risen by 31 per cent since the start of 2020.[6] We pay almost a third more for food. Food commodity prices have also risen by a third. And, as with most of the impacts of climate change, the price is being paid by the people who can least afford it, not just in Germany, Britain, or here in Belgium. But also – and especially – in the southern hemisphere.

~ ~ ~

The UN's July 2023 report on world hunger reveals that nearly half of the global population cannot afford adequate nutritious food. As many as 3.1 billion people cannot access enough fruit and vegetables. As a result, the UN's Sustainable Development Goals to eradicate hunger by the year 2030 are in jeopardy. Instead of being

5 World Economic Forum, 'Record temperatures are driving food prices higher. Here are some of the crops facing the biggest impacts', 9 August 2023.
6 Food and Agriculture Organisation of the United Nations, 3 February 2023.

hunger-free, the world will have 600 million people suffering from chronic malnutrition that year.[7]

Everyone involved is sounding the alarm. Olivier De Schutter, UN special rapporteur on extreme poverty and human rights, doesn't mince his words: 'What an indictment of our failing food system! It's not that the world is not producing enough food. Global agriculture has never produced so many calories – its growth outpacing population growth. The industrial food system is simply not delivering. It prioritises market demand and profit over meeting human needs'.[8]

Countries in the Global South have been forced to specialise in producing easily marketable export crops like cacao, coffee, and cotton to earn the dollars needed to repay their debt. We will cover that topic in more detail later in this book. But this is at the expense of growing food for their own people. 'It is unforgivable for governments to watch billions of people going hungry in a world of plenty, as they put the interests of mega-rich agribusinesses and energy companies before those of the most vulnerable people and widen the inequality gap'. These are the words of Hanna Saarinen, Oxfam International's food policy lead.[9]

~~~

Climate disruption and war are not the only causes of high food prices. As organisations such as Greenpeace and Foodwatch International have been insisting for years, speculation also plays a significant role.

'Whenever something happens in the world, it leads to panic,

7 Food and Agriculture Organisation of the United Nations, '122 million more people pushed into hunger since 2019 due to multiple crises, reveals UN report', 12 July 2023.
8 Olivier De Schutter, 'Ons industrieel voedselsysteem hongert mensen uit', De Wereld Morgen, 8 August 2023.
9 Oxfam International, 'Oxfam reaction to the UN Global Hunger report: ending hunger is possible but requires bold collective action', 12 July 2023.

hoarding, and wild price swings', explains Lebanese Canadian professor Michael Fakhri, UN special rapporteur on the right to food. 'After Russia invaded, 7 million metric tons of Ukrainian grain could no longer be exported. This represents barely 0.9 per cent of global production. Yet grain prices rose by 70 per cent. Not so much because of that little extra supply and demand but because of market speculation. In recent years, we have begun to look at food more and more as an investment'.[10]

Olivier De Schutter shares this view. He attributes 40 per cent of the staggering food price increases in the first four months of the war to speculation. 'A handful of major financial players posted record profits during that period because they shrewdly gambled on a price increase they themselves caused through their bets'.[11] Greenpeace's research unit concludes that ten hedge funds made an estimated $1.9 billion profit by capitalising on the rise in food prices in the immediate aftermath of Russia's invasion of Ukraine.[12] Regulators in Chicago, Paris, and London allowed these financial shenanigans to continue unabated instead of preventing or curbing them.

The speculators are not interested in wheat, corn, or soy. Their interest lies in short-term profits. So, they anticipate price trends and bet on the future', explains Olivier De Schutter. 'The markets trigger speculative bubbles. That is the main explanation for the rise in food prices in world markets'.[13]

~ ~ ~

10 Caroline de Gruyter, 'We zijn voedsel steeds meer als een belegging gaan zien', *NRC.nl*, 17 April 2023

11 Maurizio Sadutto and Simon Bourgeois, 'La spéculation boursière sur les céréales a contribué à la hausse des prix de nos courses', *RTBF*, 20 February 2023.

12 Alice Ross and Margot Gibbs, 'Top hedge funds made $1.9 bn on grains ahead of the Ukraine war food price spike', *Greenpeace Unearthed*, 14 April 2023.

13 *humundi: SOS Faim*, 'Rétrospective: la Covid-19, la guerre en Ukraïne, et l'appât des spéculateurs', 14 May 2023.

Jean Wart, from Huy, knows all about speculation ravaging grain markets. As head of the agricultural cooperative Société Coopérative Agricole de la Meuse, one of the biggest grain traders in Wallonia, he sells some of his farmers' grain on the market. He vividly recalls how, in the weeks following the start of the war in Ukraine, speculators suddenly stormed the grain market. 'Like vultures over a carcass', he remarks. 'If they smell something tempting, they swoop down and speculate: up or down. These are not physical players like us'.

Jean Wart points to the warm, sweet-smelling mountain of wheat behind him. 'We will never sell anything other than what we physically have in our silos at any given time. But they only buy and sell papers, not physical grain. Step by step, I've watched them grow more powerful. Today, they represent 80 per cent of the futures market. They simply exert more and more influence'.[14] So how did grain merchants like Jean Wart become almost marginal in the market? Grain has always been traded and has always been subject to speculation. Crops such as wheat, rice and corn are sold on the exchange, as are oil, bauxite, and other commodities. Farmers, cooperatives, and agro-industrial processors are joined by financial competitors at the grain exchanges, trading thousands of virtual metric tons of grain. It's not only harvests that are traded but also promises to buy future harvests. Promises that are, in turn, resold. Today, a grain of corn can change hands up to 135 times before it reaches the end user.

By the end of the nineteenth century, with industrial capitalism in full swing, competitors had accumulated enough capital to speculate extensively. It wasn't about an ounce here and a pound there. People immediately bought warehouses and full shiploads to influence prices. The largest market for agricultural commodities, the Chicago Mercantile Exchange, was subject to

14 Maurizio Sadutto and Simon Bourgeois, 'La spéculation boursière sur les céréales a contribué à la hausse des prix de nos courses', *RTBF*, 20 February 2023.

strict regulation from 1900. Tighten the screws, was the message. For example, the Grain Futures Act of 1922 stipulated that futures trading – trading in crops that have yet to be grown – was possible on specifically approved exchanges. Transparency was also the name of the game, with all traders required to report daily. Access to the grain exchange was closely monitored; not just anyone could enter. Competitors who had nothing to do with agricultural commodities were restricted. The aim was clear: counter excessive speculation to prevent high price volatility.

All that changed in the tumultuous 1980s when the neoliberal zealots imposed their new order. Supervision was reduced, and rules were phased out. We call it deregulation. In my first book, *Op Mensenmaat (On a Human Scale)* from 2009, I explained how deregulation facilitated the financial bubbles that led us straight into the 2008 banking crisis. Under the administration of US President Bill Clinton, the hero of international social democracy at the time, barriers between savings banks and investment banks were dismantled, creating more and more room for the wildest financial players and products.[15] The same happened in the agricultural commodities market during this period. Protective rules were completely reshaped. Banks could now also trade in derivatives.

Derivatives are investment instruments. Banks, pension funds, and other large financial institutions create them to generate even more profit. Derivatives are derivative products. With derivatives, your investment is not in the value of a product but in a derivative of that product. Futures are a specific type of derivative. You are buying products that have yet to be made. For example, a grain company can sell its crop for a certain price long before it is harvested. That's a wager. After all, the company doesn't know yet whether the harvest will be good or bad. It's also unaware of future market conditions and other related factors. It's speculating.

In 2000, the Clinton administration passed the Commodity

15 Peter Mertens, *Op Mensen Maat: Stof voor een socialisme zonder blauwe plekken*, EPO, Berchem, 2009, pp. 52-53.

Futures Modernisation Act. The new law exempted trading in agricultural derivatives from the market regulator's oversight. Purely speculative trading in derivatives and futures was then allowed. With this law, President Clinton opened the stock market to all manner of financial sharks: flash traders using fast computers and smart algorithms to take advantage of price differences that exist for a fraction of a second; speculators betting on price movements if grain becomes scarce due to drought, boycotts, or war; and traders in multiple repackaged derivatives trading grain they don't have, don't want, and never will want.

Since Clinton's modernisation laws, legions of pension funds, private equity firms, hedge funds, and sovereign wealth funds have descended on the agricultural temple, all looking for quick profits. Japan's public pension fund and the California state employees' pension fund are among the largest institutional investors. Money from the people's own pension, thanks to pension privatisation, is being used to speculate on food prices. You couldn't make this up.

Deregulation and liberalisation create tremendous price fluctuations, which is exactly what the Grain Futures Act of 1922 was designed to avoid. Extreme price instability causes food crises. We have seen it happen several times over the past few decades. Food riots have broken out from Egypt to Haiti and Bangladesh to Mexico.

'Hunger is not a death sentence'. Swiss sociologist Jean Ziegler, almost ninety years old, has dedicated his life to addressing this issue. As the former UN Special Rapporteur on the Right to Food, he knows what he's talking about. 'To eradicate hunger, you must ban stock market speculation in basic foodstuffs. How do you do that? Quite simply: through law. No stock exchange in the world functions without law. If public pressure is strong enough, a country's parliament can introduce a new provision prohibiting stock market speculation'.[16]

16 CCFD Terre solidaire, 'Entretien avec Jean Ziegler: la voix des sans voix', *ccfd-terresolidaire.org*, 15 December 2021.

Cargill

For those who make the rules, there are no rules.
    Thomas Shelby in *Peaky Blinders*

Natural disasters make food more expensive. So does speculation. Yet, more is going on in the land of food, argues Dan Saladino, food journalist for the BBC. 'Of the 6,000 plant species humans have eaten over time, the world now mostly eats just nine, of which just three – rice, wheat and maize – provide 50 per cent of all calories. Add potato, barley, palm oil, soy, and sugar (beet and cane) and you have 75 per cent of all the calories that fuel our species'. And we get them from all over the world. Saladino's columns were recently collated in his marvellous book *Eating to Extinction*.[1]

Throughout history, humans have eaten thousands of species and varieties of plants and animals, with enormous genetic diversity adapted to local conditions. Dan Saladino claims that this diversity has disappeared in just a few decades. Most people are oblivious to this, as giant supermarkets create the illusion of overwhelming choice. But it's an industrialised form of diversity. As Saladino explains:

'We can buy all kinds of sodas and sushi whenever and wherever we want. But what we buy and eat is increasingly similar around the world. Half the world grows the same hybrid corn types used to make high fructose corn syrup for our soft drinks and feed for pigs. These pigs worldwide are

1 Dan Saladino, *Eating to Extinction. The World's Rarest Foods and Why We Need to Save Them*, Vintage Arrow Mass Market, 2023.

all the same breed – the Large White – and all other breeds are nearly extinct. Control of the world's seed production is in the hands of just four corporations, and more than half the world's cheese is made with enzymes and starter cultures from the same Danish company.'[2]

While seed banks hold 560,000 varieties of grain, a few seeds still dominate global trade. Today, a rich food culture that has developed over thousands of years is being eroded. That a handful of multinationals dominate the production and trade of our food is, in Saladino's words, 'very disturbing'. The food giants also have the power of monopoly pricing at their disposal.

Today, four titans practically control the entire food chain: from the grain in the field to the products on the shelves. The four are unknown but reign supreme. They are called 'the ABCDs', after the first letters of their company names: ADM, Bunge, Cargill, and Dreyfus. They control networks of silos, railways, and ships, and they have the data and relationships needed to map out the supply routes. They dominate 70 per cent of the grain trade and hold the largest stocks.

~~~

Take Cargill, for instance. Even if you've never heard of the company, chances are you have Cargill products in your shopping basket. Cargill buys the grain for our bread. It produces the fats in our margarine, the dextrose in jams, the ingredients in baby milk, and much more. All day long, Cargill buys, processes, and sells the ingredients of what's in our refrigerators.

These food items and ingredients are sourced from all over the world. Today, founder William Wallace Cargill's descendants own a company that operates in 125 countries: pretty much everywhere,

2 Frank Mulder, 'We eten enkel nog verpakt water', *De Groene Amsterdammer*, 15 February 2023.

in fact. This makes Cargill the world's largest trader and producer of food ingredients and agricultural products. 'We are the flour in your bread, the wheat in your noodles, and the corn in your tortillas', is one of the company's slogans. 'But, first and foremost, we're the hole in your wallet', would be a fitting addition. No fewer than 12 Cargill family members feature on *Forbes* magazine's annual billionaires list. The Cargill dozen have combined assets of $33.4 billion – their wealth has skyrocketed at a dizzying rate. Wake up one morning, go to work, go to sleep, and wake up the next day with an extra $20 million in your bank account: that's pretty much what happened to the Cargills day after day between 2020 and 2022. Their family wealth grew by $20 million a day for two years.[3] All that money comes from items in your shopping basket, and those bought by Kath, her colleagues, and millions more.

~ ~ ~

For food titans like Cargill, high prices are akin to a jackpot: a one-armed bandit. Cargill and company have a dominant position: they control the market. And they use that power in the pursuit of ever-higher returns and profit margins. *The sky's the limit*, even in an industry built around the basic need to eat.

Cargill has divided the world into production zones from its headquarters in Minnesota in the United States to palm oil in Indonesia, sunflower oil in France, grain in Ukraine, cocoa in Côte d'Ivoire, and sugar and soy in Brazil. More often than not, this monoculture causes major problems.

In the Brazilian states of Pará and Mato Grosso, for example, in the heart of the Amazon region, the landscape has undergone a dramatic transformation. Cargill's soy pirates roam the forest without wooden legs and eye patches, wrestling with nature. Now,

3 Oxfam, Profiting from Pain, 23 May 2022.

as far as the eye can see, vast fields of soybeans grow where endless forests once stood. Forests have been cut down, and local farmers' small plots have disappeared. The land where they once grew manioc, peppers, and beans has now been gobbled up by powerful soybean producers. They threaten them and set fire to their homes to take over their land. 'For us, soy is a crop of death, not life', one local farmer says. Soy from the Amazon Forest is destined for export. Soybean meal is used in animal feed for industrial feedlots in Europe. And soybean oil is turned into 'biofuel', a cynical name for a fuel two to three times more climate-damaging than fossil fuels.

To increase profit margins, Cargill is willing to play fast and loose with laws, rules, and morals. Mighty Earth, an international environmental organisation, has labelled Cargill the Worst Company in the World for its unscrupulous business practices, deforestation, and exploitation.[4] And the NGO ClientEarth has filed a legal complaint against Cargill, claiming that it bears a 'crushing responsibility for the demise of the Amazon forest'.[5]

In the spring of 2023, a labour inspection at the Cargill meatpacking plant in Dodge City, Kansas (United States), uncovered twenty-six children working there illegally for the cleaning service that operates in slaughterhouses throughout the country. The inspectors found that children were required to work with hazardous chemicals and to clean equipment such as back saws, brisket saws, and head splitters. Some of them had to spend the night in the slaughterhouse; others were injured while working.

This is not the jungle of Chicago at the start of the last century: the Chicago of the meat kings and the appalling living and working conditions of slaughterhouse workers, as Upton Sinclair depicted them in the ground-breaking novel *The Jungle* (1905). This is the United States today. The labour inspector found that the

4 'Cargill: The Worst Company In the World', *Mighty Earth*, 11 July 2019.
5 Ine Renson, 'Ook voor Belgische kaas en Hamburgers wordt regenwoud gekapt', *De Standaard Weekend*, 3 June 2023.

child labour ban violations were 'systemic', 'reached across eight states', and clearly indicated 'a corporate-wide failure at all levels'. The cleaning company got off with a fine. Meanwhile, the Cargill jackpot family counts its profits.

~~~

The Cargills of this world, the 25 global food industry heavyweights, collectively profited to the tune of a staggering $155 billion in 2021. By the next year, that figure was even higher.[6] So, their shareholders are making a killing on food prices. No wonder *Forbes* has listed 62 more food billionaires in the last two years. They now number 245 and have seen their combined assets grow by 45 per cent over the past two years.[7] 'Food companies are taking advantage of this very precarious moment', says Irit Tamir, Director of Oxfam America. 'They are hiding behind a very good story of the pandemic, inflation, and the Ukraine war to say that they need to raise prices, but they are actually just creating a smash and grab for profit, exploiting and exacerbating inflation.'[8]

6 Chloe Sorvino, 'Forbes Global 2000: The World's Largest Food Companies In 2022', *Forbes*, 12 May 2022.
7 Oxfam, Profiting from pain. The urgency of taxing the rich amid a surge in billionaire wealth and a global cost-of-living crisis, May 2022.
8 Nik Popli, 'How Food Companies' Massive Profits Are Making Your Groceries More Expensive', *Time*, 6 April 2023.

The Two-Hundred-Billion-Dollar Men

Riches are like muck,
they stink in a heap,
but, spread abroad,
make the earth fruitful.
            Francis Bacon, 1625

March 2023. In major cities across Belgium, we have teamed up with Medicine for the People's health centres to set up energy kiosks. Energy prices have soared, and we want to guide people through the maze of the market and bills. Hundreds of people seek advice. We also use energy cafés to go on the road and help people understand why prices are high and what we need to do to change them.

Emma enters our energy kiosk in the Belgian city of Seraing. She is at a loss for words. Her final bill has arrived in the mail. She has to cough up an additional €1,500 and has no idea how to pay for it. A repayment plan? After paying current bills and expenses, she's hardly left with anything. Emma confides that she has put a little money aside. But now she has to make a choice. She hesitates. Not pay the bill? Put off the specialist's appointment again? The minor remodelling of her house? Or the vet for her cat? She simply doesn't know.

Emma isn't the only one. Since autumn 2022, almost every occupational group has been sounding the alarm. All sorts of politicians are on television giving energy-saving tips. Christian Leysen, successful manager of shipping company Ahlers and Anacom distribution and MP for the Open VLD (The Open

Flemish Liberals and Democrats), even brings a thick scarf to the plenary session of the Chamber of Representatives: to show Belgians how it should be done. I let fly at the session: 'It's not about tips to turn down the heating or wear an extra pullover. People are already doing that. The government shouldn't be giving people tips they're already implementing. It needs to come up with solutions. Because people are drowning'.

It's not only the food giants and supermarket chains imposing high prices. Energy companies like power giant Engie Electrabel did the same in 2022. Around €35 per megawatt hour: that's how much it costs Engie Electrabel to produce electricity at its Belgian nuclear power plants. For years, Engie has sold its nuclear power at an average of €50 per megawatt hour – an extremely healthy margin because the nuclear plants have long since been paid off. Gas prices soared when Russia invaded Ukraine. Not because of a shortage of gas, but because speculators were betting on possible future shortages, as we'll see later in this book. War or no war, it still costs Engie €35 per megawatt hour to produce electricity. But because electricity prices are linked to gas prices, they also skyrocket. Engie can suddenly sell its electricity at double, triple, or quadruple the price without spending or investing a cent more. This allows Engie to make additional profits on top of its normal profit margin: surplus profits.

~~~

It is a beautiful Sunday afternoon when Tim saunters into our home in Linkeroever. Our garage is being used as a temporary storage area for the party section in our neighbourhood, and Tim has come to pick up the borrowed fridge. Tim has a voice like a cathedral bell, as clear as it is powerful. He has worked in the petroleum industry all his life and is a union veteran. This towering guy with an Antwerp accent and gentle nature makes it his business to involve and inform everyone in the workplace as much as possible.

When he talks about his union work at our kitchen table that Sunday, I notice how many millions roll off his tongue. Because the oil industry is not about hundreds or thousands. That's 'small change'. In petroleum, where the scale of things is not big, but truly gigantic, they talk about millions. Five giants control the oil market: ExxonMobil, Shell, TotalEnergies, Chevron, and BP. Together, they represent Big Oil. The Big Five control oil refining. They know how to impose their prices on the market.

It does them no harm. They've posted considerable profits over the past five years. But what happened in 2022 trumps everything. The Big Five recorded the biggest profits in their history: two hundred billion dollars. This staggering number is almost impossible to grasp. Two hundred billion dollars in profits for just five companies. News reports mention the number, but not much else, moving quickly on to the next item, such as the birth of a seal at the zoo and treating the eye-popping profit figures as no more than routine news.

Energy consumers are footing the bill for obscene profits while stories of energy poverty abound at our energy kiosks and cafés.

'What isn't oil in?', Tim asks himself. And he begins ticking off the list: 'Almost all plastic or synthetic objects are made from oil. Your smartphone case, laptop keyboard, any clothing made of polyester or nylon, your bicycle, hospital testing equipment, you name it'. Virtually every manufacturing process requires energy, and many industrial processes use oil as a raw material, for instance, to make plastics. So, exorbitant energy prices are leaving a wide trail of price increases in their wake. Surplus profits in oil are also driving up other prices.

'As millions struggle to heat their homes and put food on the table', says British union leader Paul Nowak, 'BP is laughing all the way to the bank'. The British oil company BP made record profits of nearly $28 billion in 2022. France's TotalEnergies sees profits of $36 billion roll in – another record. ExxonMobil posts the largest annual profit ever made by an oil company: $56 billion. Money seems to fall from the sky like manna from heaven.

The oil companies haven't earned surplus profits, protests Nobel laureate economist Joseph Stiglitz. He calls them *windfall profits*, profits that come to you without any effort on your part.[1] This windfall profit is then juxtaposed with unprecedentedly high energy bills and prices at the petrol pump for ordinary people. They are less fortunate.

~~~

Nearly all the shops in rue du Collège in Verviers are closed. Many houses are boarded up, and the streets echo with the hum of large fans, blowing the humid air dry. One year after the Vesder floods, debris and car wrecks still litter the area. Thousands of families were forced to leave their homes, and 41 people lost their lives on the day unprecedented rainfall inundated the Vesder Valley.

I've been with our SolidarisTeams volunteers a few times now to pump out the houses and help people. The smell of damp and heating oil is inescapable, but the solidarity of thousands of helpers is heart-warming. Mother Nature has wreaked havoc in the Vesder Valley. No one can deny that global warming is causing extreme weather events. And it's the less fortunate who are paying the price.

According to the International Energy Agency, the world couldn't afford any new oil drilling projects after 2021; otherwise, limiting global warming to the threshold of 1.5°C would become unattainable. That was leaving aside the explosion of windfall profits. Eager to still take full advantage of super-high prices, Big Oil has been funding new fossil fuel investments between 2022 and

---

1 'Joseph Stiglitz, US economist: Companies making windfall profits', *Agence-France Presse*, 19 September 2022.

2023 to the tune of $140 billion. 'Moral and economic madness' is what UN Secretary-General António Guterres calls it, and he is right.

Pakistan was hit hard in 2022. First came a period of drought and a heat wave with temperatures reaching 51°C, followed by heavy monsoon rains in September that flooded a quarter of the country. Multiply the Vesder Valley floods by a thousand, and you have an idea of the deluges in Pakistan. Two thousand people died, and millions more have been displaced or are clearing debris. With under $15 billion of its 2022 surplus profits alone, BP could cover the flood damage in Pakistan and still be left with four to five billion dollars in surplus profits. That's on top of the $9 billion in normal profits.

Isn't using these surplus profits to cover the consequences of fossil fuels an obvious choice? It doesn't happen. Instead, more than half of the historic two-hundred-billion-dollar windfall profit is going to the richest shareholders. Big Oil's big five will pay their shareholders $48 billion in dividends in 2022. And they are driving up share prices by buying $54 billion of their own shares.[2] You need a magnifying glass to look for investments in renewable energy.

BP decided to adjust its plans to cut 40 per cent of emissions by 2030 to just 25 per cent. Even Shell has no intention of increasing its investment in renewables. And at both ExxonMobil and Chevron, shareholders voted against proposals to do more for the climate. They would rather enjoy big dividends in the years to come. Big Oil: not good for your wallet, a disaster for the climate.

2 'Crisis year 2022 brought $134 billion in excess profit to the West's five largest oil and gas companies', *Global Witness*, 9 February 2023.

Prices and Profits

It is difficult to get a man to understand something when his salary depends on his not understanding it.
  Upton Sinclair

Monopoly prices and speculation on gas, grain, and food prices by oil and food giants: these are the main drivers of the price increases in 2022. Yet by the end of the year, politicians, business leaders, and economists are all in thrall to the idea that it's mainly wages that are driving up prices. In every country in Europe, the bigwigs are talking about the danger of the wage-price spiral: the fear that higher wages will lead to higher prices.

In 1996, in the run-up to the introduction of the euro, the 'Roman-Red' government in Belgium of Jean-Luc Dehaene (1992-1999), so-called for being a coalition between the Catholic and social-democratic parties, introduced the Salaries and Wages Act. Politics intervened in wages. Typically, politicians shout down any attempt for legislative bills to significantly affect pricing. But when it comes to political intervention in setting wages, the leading circles make less fuss. The Salaries and Wages Act restricts free wage bargaining and authorises the government to freeze wage increases for two-year periods, in line with developments in neighbouring countries. In 2017, the government led by Charles Michel (2014-2019), with the Liberals, Christian Democrats, and the New Flemish Alliance (N-VA), made the Act even stricter. The policy wants our wages to move slower than in neighbouring countries: a downward wage spiral. That leaves room for wage increases of barely 0.4 per cent above inflation for 2021-2022, and even 0 per cent for 2023-2024 – nothing, in other words. According to the

National Bank, real wages in Belgium fell 1.79 per cent in 2021 and 2.13 per cent in 2022.[1] In 2020, four parties with a range of different views – the Liberals (Open Flemish Liberals and Democrats and the Reformist Movement), the Social Democrats (Vooruit and Socialist Party), the Greens (Groen and Ecolo), and the Christian Democrats (CD&V, Christian Democratic and Flemish) – came together to form the Vivaldi Coalition (named after Vivaldi's Four Seasons). Despite the election promises of the social democrats and the Greens, the Vivaldi government has not changed the draconian wage law. The unions are unhappy about this. With petitions, various forms of strike action and large demonstrations, they are waging a long battle to have the law revised. No end is yet in sight. They've announced that they will keep up the pressure until wage negotiations are again free in Belgium.

So, how do wages drive up prices? While wages are in negative territory, it's hard to say the same for prices. Even so, newspaper headlines continue to cling to the old spectre of the wage-price spiral. The sermon about how rising wages drive up prices is repeated *ad nauseam*. As the saying goes, if you want to fight price rises, you need to preach wage moderation. In the autumn of 2022, Christine Lagarde (president of the European Central Bank); Andrew Bailey (governor of the Bank of England); German Chancellor Olaf Scholz; French President Emmanuel Macron; Klaas Knot (president of DNB, the Dutch central bank); and Pierre Wunsch (governor of the National Bank of Belgium), all warned against the spectre of the wage-price spiral.

~~~

Six economists from the International Monetary Fund asked what historical evidence there is of wage-price spirals. They decided to investigate the matter in more depth. They acted

1 National Bank of Belgium, Economic projections for Belgium, June 2022.

diligently, reviewing all the wage and price details of thirty-one countries with advanced economies, including Belgium, for the entire period from 1960 to 2021. Their findings are surprising: there is little evidence of the much-feared spiral in the data for those sixty years. And while there have been short periods of rising wages and rising prices, it is rare for prices and wages to drive each other up over a long period. In conclusion, wage-price spirals exist, but they are rare. [2]

So, what does drive prices up? Isabella Weber, a German economist, studies how prices rise after periods of economic shock, such as at the end of World War I or World War II, when the wartime economy, churning out tanks and shells, suddenly had to switch to producing cars and vacuum cleaners – quite a change! Weber's research shows that large firms and robust sectors are able to continue raising prices in the market unless the government intervenes after such a shock, for example, by regulating prices. The COVID stoppage is a similar economic shock, Weber argues. She notes that in the search for the cause of post-pandemic price increases, one factor has been routinely overlooked: big business's record-high profit margins. Not only were higher energy costs passed on, but the opportunity was also seized to boost profits. Isabella Weber made this connection in a powerful opinion piece in *The Guardian* and argued for price controls.[3]

And that's when the show began. Reaction to Weber's study has been uncommonly harsh. Suggesting price controls equates to blasphemy in the Orthodox economic church. The high priests of traditional economics condemned Weber. Price intervention is outside-the-box thinking. The dominant economics profession ignores Weber, clinging doggedly to its old views. As always, the

2 Jorge A. Alvarez, John C. Bluedorn, Niels-Jakob H. Hansen et al, 'Wage-Price Spirals: What is the Historical Evidence?', IMF Working Papers 22/221, 11 November 2022.

3 Isabella Weber, 'Could strategic price controls help fight inflation?' *The Guardian*, 29 December 2021.

finger of blame is pointed at wages and trade unions. The notion that profit margins can drive up prices is dismissed as being purely driven by 'emotion'. The governor of the Dutch central bank, Klaas Knot, repeated it three times on public television: 'Emotion!'.[4]

~~~

The facts prove Knot is wrong and Weber is right. The profit-price spiral and not the wage-price spiral is the main culprit. Economist Michael Roberts worked for more than four decades at the heart of global capitalism in the City of London. He is at odds with central bankers and mainstream experts: 'First, inflation remains "sticky" not because wage rises (or spending) from labour have been excessive. After the pandemic, the poor recovery in output and productivity coupled with a very slow return to international transport of raw materials and components kicked off the inflationary spiral – not workers demanding higher wages'. Roberts argues further: 'If anything, it is excessive profits that have driven up prices. Taking advantage of supply chain blockages after the COVID pandemic and shortages of critical materials, multi-national energy, food, and communications companies raised prices to reap higher profits'.[5]

The buzzword is *greedflation*, implying that companies have greedily hiked the margin between costs and prices to boost profits. But big business is always in search of higher profit margins. It is no greedier today than it was yesterday. And so, Isabella Weber does not use the term greedflation. She links rising prices to the rebound of the economy and steadfastly speaks of sellers' inflation.

No matter what you call the beast, research institution after research institution is finding compelling evidence that profits play

4 Klaas Knot in Buitenhof, NPO, 7 May 2023.
5 Michael Roberts, 'From greedflation to stagflation and then slumpflation', *The Next Recession*, 5 July 2023.

a significant role in driving up prices. Everyone has reached the same conclusion, from the Federal Reserve Bank of Kansas City to the economists at Goldman Sachs.[6] The European Central Bank's research department is no exception. According to its calculations, two-thirds of price increases in 2022 were driven by higher profit margins.[7] Belgian think tank Minerva says the same: from every euro more for a product, nearly twenty cents go to higher profit margins and only ten cents to higher wages.[8] The final blow for the doubters came on 26 June 2023, when the International Monetary Fund tweeted: 'Rising corporate profits account for almost half the increase in Europe's inflation over the past two years as companies increased prices by more than spiking costs of imported energy'.[9] Emotion, Mr. Knot?

Of course, the big question behind the whole debate is who will bear the cost of rising prices. This is what is at stake in the coming battles. Will big business have to cut back on its historically high-profit margins, as Isabella Weber and others contend? Or will high prices be passed on to the working class?

'Economists treat inflation as a neutral, objective fact. Something that just happens. And it's up to central banks to stop it. But it's not. Inflation is a very political phenomenon', Grace Blakeley tells me. 'The balance of costs and benefits and their distribution reflect the prevailing power relations in a society. Who bears the cost of inflation depends on who holds the power

6 Andrew Glover, José Mustre-del-Río and Alice von Ende-Becker, 'How Much Have Record Corporate Profits Contributed to Recent Inflation', Federal Reserve Bank of Kansas City, 12 January 2023 and Christian Schnittker, 'European Economics Analyst The Role of Profit Margins in Euro Area Inflation', Goldman Sachs, 19 April 2023.
7 Oscar Arce, Elke Hahn and Gerrit Koester, 'How tit-for-tat inflation can make everyone poorer', European Central Bank, 30 March 2022.
8 Matthias Somers, 'Lonen, prijzen, winsten: een analyse van de bedrijfsresultaten in tijden van inflatie', *Minerva Think Tank*, 26 October 2022.
9 International Monetary Fund, 'Europe's Inflation Outlook Depends on How Corporate Profits Absorb Wage Gains', 26 June 2023.

in that society. Before they allow inflation to impinge on their bottom line, businesses and corporations will always try to pass costs on to workers, and after workers, to consumers'.

Chapter 2

Recession Therapy

The Ever Given

We sail for a sailor's wage
across the salty sea!
Although no women ever come along
across the briny, across the salty sea!
Whether our spirits are high or low
across the salty sea!
We are blown by the wind
across the briny, across the salty sea!
Wannes Van de Velde, *Bitter Sailor's Song.*

Climate, war, and speculation all push up prices. As does the market clout of the oil and food giants. But prices started to rise earlier than that: when the economy stuttered back to life at the end of the COVID-19 lockdowns. To get a better picture, let's zoom in on an ancient conduit between east and west: the Suez Canal.[1]

Fierce desert winds have painted the sky yellow. Through the dust, Captain Krishnan Kanthavel can see the sun rising over the Red Sea. His vessel, the *Ever Given*, is anchored in the Gulf of Suez with 224,000 tonnes of cargo, waiting to begin the 12-hour passage through the Suez Canal. The experienced shipmaster from Tamil Nadu, India, knows what lies ahead is no picnic. Although it saves a three-week voyage around Africa, the canal is just 24 metres deep and 200 metres wide. He will have to steer his 400-metre beast through it with the help of local canal pilots.

1 The story of the *Ever Given* blocking the canal is based on *Bloomberg's* excellent reporting: Kit Chellel, Matthew Campbell, and K Oanh Ha, 'Six Days in Suez: The Inside Story of the Ship That Broke Global Trade', *Bloomberg*, 24 June 2021.

Carrying 17,600 containers, the keel of the *Ever Given* is only a few metres above the canal floor. Captain Kanthavel knows that there is no margin for error. The pilots and ship's management briefly disagree over whether the vessel can proceed. The weather is bad. The day before, the captain of a Qatari gas tanker decided it was too stormy to risk the passage. Four ports in the area have already closed today. But Captain Kanthavel is feeling the pressure. It is huge. His cargo is worth about a billion dollars. Every day of delay is costly. The containers must arrive in the port of Rotterdam as soon as possible. What follows is world news.

Barely a few miles up the canal, the beast begins to sway erratically from port to starboard and back again. The ship's massive hull makes quick course corrections exceedingly difficult. With hundreds of thousands of tonnes of water crammed between the hull and the shore, all the laws of physics come to life. Deep below the waterline, the bulging bow bores into the sand and rocks, and the stern also runs aground. It is around 7:40 am on Tuesday, 23 March 2021. The *Ever Given* is lodged at a 45-degree angle to the shore in one of the worst places imaginable, a one-way stretch of the canal. No other vessel can pass; the Suez Canal is blocked.

After a day, 185 ocean-going vessels – full of electronics, cement, water, and oil – are already waiting impatiently in a long traffic jam. Up to four hundred container ships will eventually be involved in the largest maritime congestion in history. Now, the pressure is on the highly specialised sea tugs, barges, and dredgers. It is only after six days of dredging, pulling, and tugging that they manage to free the *Ever Given*. Some 30,000 cubic metres of sand were dredged for this purpose. A photograph of a lone excavator goes viral worldwide.

Connecting the east and west of our planet, the Suez Canal is the artery of world trade. Nine billion dollars' worth of goods pass daily from the Red Sea to the Mediterranean and vice versa, accounting for 12 per cent of global trade in goods. The *Ever Given* canal crash illustrates how fragile the global economy has become.

~~~

What the Persians, Greeks, Romans, Arabs, Byzantines, Mongols, Chinese, Ottomans, Genoese, and Venetians had in common is that they connected cities and towns across Eurasia in a network of trade routes. Precious goods, people, and ideas have travelled along these ancient Silk Roads for centuries. The hubs of trade and encounter were the pillars upon which empires rose and fell. Port cities are commercial cities. And in such cities, the port is the city, and the city is the port. The salty smell of seafaring and merchant shipping fills every alley and bar. Antwerp has always been a city of quays, full of goods and languages. I heard Wannes Van de Velde tell of how, as a teenager, he would stand at the door of Spanish inns and listen to flamenco or watch rebetika being sung through the keyhole of Greek taverns. The city's bars were the scene of heated discussions between German, Neapolitan, Irish, and Scandinavian sailors, which invariably led to more pitchers of beer. But the port has left the city. The Zeemanshuis, where sailors used to spend the night, have disappeared from the centre. So, too has the dockers' recruiting hall, 'the Kot' in Antwerp, with dockers' cafés around it. The old port district of Het Eilandje is already becoming as gentrified as those of Rotterdam, London, and Hamburg.

Anyone who has ever walked a dock knows how tightly intertwined the global economy is today. A DNA strand is no match for this. As someone commented: whoever dips their toe in the river Scheldt is in touch with the whole world.

The container plays a pivotal role in this story. If a ship misses its scheduled arrival time, that is a problem not only for the Port of Antwerp but also for companies across the hinterland, reaching far beyond the Ruhr. Delays can also cause backlogs at other world ports. Some containers are transferred to other ships that proceed to their final destination, such as New York Harbour, after transhipment. Companies across the pond then also have to wait for raw materials or parts. Growing container shipping is part of the just-in-time (JIT) system, where inventory is eliminated, and all processes are organised so that raw materials and goods are delivered exactly where and when companies need them. The globalised, hyper-organised world of mega-ships makes this possible. The introduction of the standardised container in the 1970s was a big step in this direction. Before long, infrastructure around the world was adapted to the standard size of containers: everything from the width of rail cars and locks to the height of overpasses. Today, 90 per cent of everything you own comes from such a container: 5.9 metres long, 2.4 metres wide and 2.4 metres high.

The container is the hero of our consumer society. It's no coincidence then that the business magazine *The Economist* has paid tribute to it: 'Although only a simple metal box, it has transformed global trade. In fact, new research suggests that the container has been more of a driver of globalisation than all trade agreements in the past fifty years taken together'.[2]

Before the steel box came along, it could take up to a week to load or unload a large ship. We no longer count in weeks but in days, leaving sailors with very little time to go ashore. What's more, there are far fewer of them. A four-hundred-metre floating mastodon with 18,000 containers barely has twenty-five people on board. That's not many people, so many sailors' bars are deserted or have long since closed their doors. Nine major shipping companies control almost all container trade. They call the shots and define the depth of the vessels, which are getting bigger and ever more imposing. A port has to adapt to this, with new quays and docks of sufficient draught. Ships are now loaded and unloaded on large concrete pads far from city centres. Container traffic has certainly taken ports out of cities. But it has also helped boost global trade.

2 'The humble hero', *Economist*, 18 May 2013.

Containers are part of the international production chains snaking across the planet. JIT is designed to eliminate storage, inventory, and waiting costs and to increase profit margins. It is also the Achilles heel of the system: a fly in the ointment is enough to disrupt the whole chain.

~~~

Back to the *Ever Given*. It got stuck at a particularly challenging time. COVID-19 has raged around the world for two years, causing hundreds of thousands of work hours to be lost to lockdowns and plunging most countries into recession. Manufacturing sectors ground to a halt, especially where lockdowns were tight. Semiconductor production in China, for example, was shutting down, setting off a chain reaction. Because semiconductors are the building blocks of all electronic devices, both analogue and digital, from transistors, LED lamps and displays to medical electronics and aircraft control panels. In late 2021, the deadly variant of the virus was still circulating in the south of the planet. Vaccination rates there were too low, and Big Pharma was refusing to open up patents. The price for this was later be paid for not only in lives and jobs, but also with a bumpy restart of the global economy.

Europe and the United States were in total chaos that autumn. Semiconductors were needed to make computer chips for modern cars. Automakers cancelled orders for them during the lockdown. Of course, many people were working from home anyway. So, who was ordering cars? Televisions, tablets, computers, and smartphones attracted eager customers, and the electronics industry was only too happy to take orders for semiconductors. As the economy recovered, the auto industry was massively short of semiconductors, and a new wave of COVID-19 was sweeping across Asia, where computer chips are made. Waiting lists for cars grew longer, auto workers were put on temporary unemployment, and car prices skyrocketed. Amid this chaos, even the slightest hiccup was enough to make the economy's engine sputter and send prices soaring. During the pandemic, dockworkers at US ports were laid off due to the lack of activity. They went to work elsewhere. When the economy picked up, there was a shortage of dockworkers and waiting times at the ports increased.

Newspaper headline, November 2021:

'Nightmare around the port of Los Angeles: shipping containers crush cars and block access to homes'.[3]

There was no space to stack containers at the largest port in the United States right before Christmas. You would never believe it, but they were all over the city. It was a crazy sight: large walls of containers towering over houses and electricity poles. Locals were starting to lose it. What on earth was going on? As the economy improved, there were not enough dockworkers and truck drivers to get everything out on time. Off the coast of California, ships carrying hundreds of thousands of tonnes of goods had to wait to dock. Goods become more expensive.

Major shipping companies responded to the delays by drastically raising transportation prices, which was ultimately passed on to consumers. In the autumn of 2021, sending a container from Shanghai to Antwerp costs seven times as much as the year before. The following year, the ten largest shipping companies in the world made an estimated profit of – wait for it – $223 billion. These are the same astronomical amounts as in the oil sector: numbers too large for the human brain to assimilate.

The world's fragile just-in-time supply chains pushed inflation up to 4 per cent by October 2021. This is the first phase of price increases, months before the outbreak of the war in Ukraine.

~ ~ ~

3 Jan Postma, 'Nachtmerrie rond haven Los Angeles: zeecontainers pletten auto's en blokkeren huizen', *De Telegraaf*, 8 November 2021.

This means that we've gone through three phases of continued price rises: the first was the sputtering restart after COVID-19; the second was the mega-profits shamelessly passed on in prices; and the third phase was where food prices, in particular, remained stubbornly high.

In this second chapter, we examine the policy response. Why is so much emphasis being put on interest rate hikes? We also look at the consequences of that choice: ballooning debt, profiteering banks, shadow banks, and the wave of austerity looming over us.

Thatcher Therapy

For theirs is a land with a wall around it
And mine is a faith in my fellow man
Theirs is a land of hope and glory
Mine is the green field and the factory floor
    Billy Bragg, *Between the Wars*

Since Rishi Sunak took over the prime ministership of the UK in October 2022, his task has been to fight inflation and pull his country's ailing economy out of the doldrums. The millionaire climbed into the saddle, backed by the City, the financial heart of London. Sunak had said in his campaign, 'I am running as a Thatcherite, and I will govern as a Thatcherite'. A Thatcherite is a supporter of the right-wing Conservative prime minister of the 1980s, Margaret Thatcher. Meanwhile, the British press was eager to talk about Thatcher's 'recession therapy'. And those voices can also be heard popping up elsewhere. But what is Thatcher's therapy?

In June 1992, the BBC broadcast the third episode of *Pandora's Box*, an economic history documentary series by Adam Curtis.[1] Watching this episode today transports you back to the early nineties when colour television had yet to mature, and the screen was still as square as the heavy TV sets of yesteryear. Fifteen minutes into the BBC documentary, Sir Alan Budd appears, a balding, bearded man, in a dapper suit with a polka-dot tie. Compared to the bulky computers flickering behind him in the exhibition building, he looks modern. Though he bears a passing

1 BBC, Pandora's Box – Part 3: 'The League of Gentlemen', 22 June 1992.

resemblance to Lenin, Sir Alan Budd is no lefty. While working at the London Business School in the 1970s, he quickly became an evangelist for Milton Friedman's neoliberal teachings. Budd went on to become an advisor to the Bank of England. According to insiders, he played a major role behind the scenes during the Thatcher years. In *Pandora's Box*, the professor is asked how he looks back on the Bank of England's interest rate hikes in the early 1980s, at the outset of the Thatcher era, increases that led to unprecedented unemployment and the destruction of the UK's industrial centres. Documentary filmmaker Adam Curtis conducts the interview.

ADAM CURTIS: For some economists who were involved in this story, there is a further question: were their theories used to disguise political policies that would have otherwise been very difficult to implement in Britain?

ALAN BUDD: The nightmare I sometimes have about this whole experience, runs as follows. I was involved in making a number of proposals which were partly at least adopted by the government and put in play by the government. Now, my worry is as follows – that there may have been people making the actual policy decisions, or people behind them or people behind them, who never believed for a moment that this was the correct way to bring down inflation. They did, however, see that it would be a very, very good way to raise unemployment, and raising unemployment was an extremely desirable way of reducing the strength of the working classes.

Although Alan Budd remains cautious, what he says is clear. A number of people in the British establishment at the time viewed raising interest rates as a 'very, very good way' to raise unemployment. And that was 'an extremely desirable way' to break the back of the working class.

A mere mortal is then faced with the question: what do price increases and interest rate hikes have to do with the strength of the working class? Let's see.

~~~

Margaret Thatcher came to power in May 1979 at a time of rampant inflation. The 1973 Arab oil embargo against the United States has triggered these price increases. The embargo is a response to US military support for Israel in that year's Yom Kippur War. It drives up oil prices, and other prices soon follow. To make matters worse, the economic engine is also sputtering. The combination of inflation and a faltering economy is unprecedented. Isn't inflation part of growth? A new word, stagflation, is already emerging. So, how do you address stagflation? Economists are at a loss.

Our time has come, thinks Milton Friedman, head of the radical liberal Chicago School of Economics. His theory is still a fringe one, as are the ideas of his Austrian brother-in-arms, Friedrich Hayek. Friedman and Hayek's call to transfer all power to banks, stock exchanges, and markets is seen as foolish by ideologues. 'Only a crisis produces real change. When that crisis occurs, the actions that are taken depend on the ideas that are lying around'. 'The politically impossible becomes the politically inevitable'. Friedman and Hayek find their holy grail in the 1973 oil crisis. Their radical ideas have matured in dozens of think tanks. Free the market from government intervention; abolish the regulations that control banks, stock exchanges, and commerce; privatise health care and education; eliminate the top tax brackets for high earners; dismantle public housing programmes; make society disappear and attribute all problems to individual failure or personal success.

These prescriptions become open to discussion in the early 1970s. The scissors are brought out to open up markets in the global south and privatise the public sector. The financial industry is given unprecedented space to tap into new areas and win markets. Friedman and his friends provide the theoretical foundations of what is known as neoliberalism today. This is no break with capitalism; it's a new phase of capitalism to respond to falling profit rates.

~~~

Something else needs to be broken to push through the neoliberal prescriptions: the prevailing consensus. This consensus was born at the end of the Second World War when no one wanted to return to the wretched crisis of the 1930s, full of social misery.

On 5 July 1945, the Labour Party brought about a major political shift in the United Kingdom. It won the election on a radical programme of social investment and nationalisation. Something similar happened in Sweden and Norway. Socialists and Communists formed coalition governments and introduced modern social security systems in France, Belgium, and Italy. Prices were capped, markets were regulated, and trade unions became a factor. This created a new balance of power between capital and labour in the three decades after the war.

You can say a lot about Margaret Thatcher, but she didn't keep her goals under wraps. On 1 May 1981, after exactly two years at the helm of the United Kingdom, she gave a mid-term review in the *Sunday Times*: 'What's irritated me about the whole direction of politics in the last 30 years is that it's always been towards the collectivist society'. The solidarity of the working class bothered her. 'And therefore, it isn't that I set out on economic policies; it's that I set out really to change the approach, and changing the economics is the means of changing that approach. If you change the approach, you really are after the heart and soul of the nation. Economics is the method; the object is to change the heart and soul'.[2] It's hard to be blunter: collectivism must be kicked out to

2 Ronald Butt, 'Margaret Thatcher Interview for Sunday Times', *Sunday Times*, 3 May 1981.

make way for the individualism of the me-me-me society. The goal is to eliminate 'the heart and soul' of the nation."

To deal with the post-war collective consensus, we must first break the back of the unions. The Chicago boys know this. The rampant inflation of the 1970s offers them a prime opportunity. In a shrewd marketing strategy, they attribute price increases to what they call 'excessive' union power, 'unreasonable' wage demands by the working class, and an 'overblown' welfare system. To put the inflationary beast back in its cage, Friedman tells the world that we need to create unemployment.

The theory goes like this. When you raise interest rates, you reduce the amount of money in the economy. Because it becomes more expensive to borrow money, it becomes harder to borrow and invest. Companies fold, and this leads to more unemployment. The more people there are competing for jobs, the more wages fall and the weaker the unions' bargaining power becomes. If people make less money, they also buy less. Then demand falls, and so do price increases, putting the inflationary beast back in its cage. It's shock therapy recession.

And what a shock it was. In 1980 and 1981, the UK plunged into the sharpest and deepest recession since the war. Private and public investment plummeted, companies folded, and manufacturing in the north of England was devastated. Three million unemployed paid the price of the therapy. Unemployment rose to more than 30 per cent in parts of the Midlands, the once-proud industrial belt. Working-class communities have yet to recover from this blow.

~ ~ ~

Economist Grace Blakeley wraps up our conversation on inflation and interest rate policy with her review of Thatcher therapy: 'The approach of triggering a recession leaves massive long-term scars which take decades to heal and for some people will never heal'. The same happened in the United States, she explained. Paul A. Volcker, chair of the Federal Reserve, doubled the base rate from 10 per cent to 20 per cent. The Volcker shock triggered a deep recession and widespread unemployment. Its scars are visible in the Rust Belt today.

Provoking recession: it is a slash-and-burn tactic with zero scruples. 'Thatcher may have put an end to the crisis of the 1970s, but she did so by plunging millions of people into poverty and creating an economy that worked for a tiny elite in the South of England'. Grace Blakeley is angry as she talks to me. 'A significant share of the political and economic turmoil through which we are living today can be traced back to the decisions made under her government'.

Living in the Red

Tax farming contracts
were publicly auctioned.
Profit was all,
and the more obscene the better.
Cities were no longer sacked,
they were bled to death instead.
   Tom Holland in *Rubicon*

Top international lawyer Richard Cooper's phone, sounds an alarm about the state of the global economy. This alarm has gone off a lot recently. As a partner at Cleary Gottlieb, a major corporate bankruptcy law firm with offices in several cities around the world, Cooper advises corporations and governments on what to do when they're drowning in debt. Cooper has survived the financial crisis and COVID-19. And he's surviving again now, in a year when large corporate bankruptcies are piling up at the second-fastest rate since 2008. This rate was surpassed only in the early days of the pandemic. 'It feels different than prior cycles', says Cooper. 'You're going to see a lot of defaults'. His position has given him a taste of the potential corporate debt storm in finance. The prospect of such a catastrophe adds to Wall Street's worries because it threatens to slow economic growth and squeeze credit markets reeling from the biggest losses in decades.

Through years of low-interest rates and unusually cheap money, debt has continued to rise. And now it's about to get a lot harder to bear because central banks have raised interest rates. Anyone trying to refinance a current debt by taking out a new loan will immediately have to pay a lot more. High interest rates are also lasting longer than Wall Street expected. Meanwhile, economic growth in Europe and China is slowing.

The first consequence of the policy decision to raise interest rates is that debt is increasing everywhere. Governments, businesses, and families have run up huge debts in recent decades. The whole of capitalism is living in the red, so to speak. Total world debt has reached $305 trillion. That's three hundred and five thousand billion dollars. And that's $45 trillion more than before the pandemic. 'It's like an elastic band', says Carla Matthews, a consultant at PricewaterhouseCoopers in the United Kingdom. 'You can keep pulling it for a while. But it will snap eventually'.

Debt isn't a big problem when productivity is high, and the economy is growing. You can repay more easily then because the pie gets bigger. But it all becomes very fragile when the economy sputters and stalls and productivity stops rising. Then, the slice of the pie that should go to interest repayments starts to get bigger and bigger. The consequence: saving. But savings also put a brake on economic growth. That's how you end up in a Catch-22 situation.

Belgium enjoyed thirty years of declining interest payments on public debt, freeing up room in the budget each year. That's over now. Market rates on long-term government bonds have already risen to the highest level of the last decade. By 2030, Belgium's government will pay an estimated six billion euros more in interest than today.

Countries of the Global South, in particular, will be under the yoke of high-interest rates. They'll have to shell out more and more money to satisfy creditors. And the more money goes to creditors, the less is left for people: for hospitals, schools, and infrastructure. Many countries are faced with an untenable situation, which is the subject of the fourth chapter of this book.

~~~

Raising interest rates will not solve any of these problems. Yet that's what central banks worldwide are doing. 'You know, Peter, the consensus since the 1980s has been that interest rates are the only tool available to policymakers in the fight against inflation'. This is how Grace Blakeley kicks off our conversation about central banks' interest rate policy. She explains how neoliberalism always views inflation as a monetary phenomenon, a money supply issue, regardless of the location. 'In short, when prices rise, it would only be because there is too much money in circulation'. The reasoning then goes like this: by raising interest rates, we make it more expensive to borrow and discourage investment. So, we limit growth and money, and prices fall. Grace Blakeley objects to this: 'This approach can work when the economy is growing fast, productivity is high, and there is willingness to invest'. Then, it might be useful to calm the economy down a bit: raise interest rates and make money more expensive. 'But we are by no means in that situation today. In fact, the uneven recovery from the pandemic, the market power of big business, and climate change are not problems you can solve by fiddling around with the cost of borrowing'.

Where this precarious situation will end up is anyone's guess. Optimists proclaim that the soft landing has already begun. Just as many doomsayers predict a huge crash. The World Bank, the European Central Bank, and the International Monetary Fund are already lowering their expectations. Oxfam has calculated that three-quarters of the world's governments are planning to cut spending over the next five years, totalling $7.8 trillion.[1]

---

1 Oxfam, 'The Commitment to Reducing Inequality Index 2022', 11 October 2022.

Banks and Shadow Banks

When one man's got a million
And another ain't got a dime
Brother, that's when law and order
Is just another name for crime
  Matt Jones, *Brother That Ain't Good*

What if theatre producers who have mastered the art of drama, suspense, and intersecting storylines were to create a podcast? Then you'd binge listen instead of binge-watch. That's what happened to me, at least, when I got to hear theatre producer Bart Van Nuffelen's podcast *De Kunst van het Verdwijnen* (The Art of Disappearing). I listened to it from start to finish. In one go. The series is about one of the most daring bank robberies in our history, which took place in Antwerp's diamond district in early 2019. The robbers entered the BNP Paribas Fortis vault through a tunnel they'd dug themselves. They made off with their spoils, valued in the millions. The spectacular tunnel heist, dryly described in the podcast as 'Aldi's Ocean's Eleven', soon becomes world news. Two of the tunnel diggers were apprehended, possibly sacrificed by the mastermind behind the robbery. As they are led into Antwerp Prison, the other inmates gave them a standing ovation. By this, I mean that bank robbers have a special status. Disgraced, sure, but admiration for daredevils who take on the banking world is never far away. A German playwright, Bertolt Brecht, once asked: 'What is robbing a bank compared to founding one?'.

Even so, the profession of bank robber seems to be on the verge of extinction, like that of a level-crossing guard or knife grinder. There are hardly any bank branches to rob in the online age.

Not that there isn't money, on the contrary. Banks seem to be doing better than ever.

Households and businesses keep their savings in private banks. These, in turn, have accounts with the national central banks within the Eurosystem, where they deposit all these savings. For that money, they now receive 3.25 per cent as the deposit facility rate from the European Central Bank. That quickly adds up to a nice sum. Today, in the summer of 2023, the commercial banks have already received €135 billion in net interest income for their reserves at the central banks.[1] Yet they are fobbing off their customers, the source of the money, with paltry interest of 1 to 1.5 per cent. And what's the result? Mega profits. Again.

'Record profits for Belgium's major banks', says a newspaper headline.[2] I read that four major Belgian banks – Belfius, BNP Paribas Fortis, KBC, and ING Belgium – recorded a combined profit of €7.3 billion in 2022 and that they're unsure what to do with all that money. Raising the savings rate is not really on the cards for now. Neither is putting enough ATMs in cities and towns. KBC announces its intention to gift €1.3 billion to its shareholders.[3] According to Paul De Grauwe, professor of economics at the London School of Economics, the interest rate policy is a subsidy policy for the banks. He writes: 'It's a disgrace. While everyone is getting worse off, the banks are getting more subsidies.'[4]

~ ~ ~

1 Wester Van Gaal, 'ECB president grilled over €135 bn interest payout to commercial banks', *EUobserver.com*, 6 June 2023.

2 Dominiek Claes, 'Recordwinsten voor Belgische grootbanken: "Ook dit jaar sterke resultaten"', *Het Belang van Limburg*, 15 March 2023.

3 Pieter Suy, 'KBC keert belegger extra 1,3 miljard euro uit', *De Tijd*, 10 August 2023.

4 Stavros Kelepouris, "Paul De Grauwe na renteverhoging ECB: 'De banken krijgen 3,25 procent, maar hun klanten geven ze nauwelijks meer dan 0 procent'", *De Morgen*, 4 May 2023.

It's as though there's nothing to worry about in banking. Maximum profits, additional subsidies through the interest rate policy... business as usual. But wait, didn't a corpse fall out of a closet somewhere in California this spring? And then again in Switzerland?

The US Silicon Valley Bank crashed on 10 March 2023. The home bank of Bay Area tech bosses and venture capitalists held $209 billion in foreign currency, making it the second-largest banking crash in US history. Silicon Valley Bank didn't hold the number two spot for long. A few weeks later, First Republic Bank also collapsed, after managing $212 billion in foreign currency.

How could this happen? For that, we need to rewind, back to the 2008 banking crisis. Massive amounts of money were pumped into the economy to revive it after the crisis. One method was a zero-interest rate policy: it cost nothing to borrow money. The flipside: money no longer earned anything, either.

As a result, financial institutions began to look for investments with slightly higher interest rates, such as long-term bonds. Here, the government or company takes out a long-term loan at a fixed rate.

Central banks have now reversed the situation with their rather abrupt interest rate rises. Suddenly, the old bonds and debt securities are not worth as much. And you get much more interest on new bonds. The result is that the banks can't unload their old bonds. Silicon Valley Bank, for example, had $90 billion, nearly half of its foreign exchange, tied up in ten-year bonds. As interest rates began to rise, these bonds lost value. The tech lender had forgotten to hedge this risk. In one fell swoop, on paper, the bank had lost nearly $16 billion.

No problem, the bankers thought, as long as none of the customers withdraw money, we'll get away with it. Until someone did. And then someone else did, and someone else, and the bank could no longer pay. That was in March 2023. Over forty billion dollars were withdrawn from accounts in two days. The tech boom was over. Many start-ups and venture capitalists desperately needed their money. Fund managers advised their clients to withdraw their money from the bank. And it happened on a massive scale, and extremely quickly. It wasn't a bank run with panicked lines of pinstriped suits at the branches. It was a digital banking sprint. Within a few hours, the bank was bankrupt.

The fact that the Trump administration, aided by many Democrats, continued to loosen banking regulations in 2018 obviously played a role in this. That's when the capital buffers for mid-sized banks were reduced, along with stress test requirements. Nor did it help that the regulator, the San Francisco Regional Federal Reserve Bank, had fallen asleep at the wheel. That might have had something to do with the fact that the CEO of Silicon Valley Bank, Greg Becker, was on the board of the San Francisco Federal Reserve. Talk about a conflict of interests!

Under US law, deposits up to $250,000 are federally insured, so if your bank fails, you get the first quarter of a million dollars back. Most mere mortals don't have that amount of money on deposit. Unless we're talking about the Bay Area. In an instant, 95 per cent of Silicon Valley Bank's deposits were no longer guaranteed. Can you imagine how insanely rich the bank's customers were! Virtually all their money was uninsured. Against all rules and agreements, the Biden administration decided that the US taxpayer should still pay to bail out the deep-pocketed venture capitalists and tech CEOs. To save Silicon Valley Bank and First Republic Bank, the US government issued $150 billion in emergency loans over one weekend.

The story is very 2008. I wrote about it then in my first book, *Op Mensenmaat*, calling for a public banking sector.[5] US economics professor Gerald Epstein is arguing for the same today: 'The recent crisis highlights a structural problem in our current financial system: there needs to be a safe place for businesses to

5 Peter Mertens, *Op Mensen Maat. Stof voor een socialisme zonder blauwe plekken*, EPO, Berchem, 2009.

place their reserves and working capital without providing funds to speculative financiers, and without fear that their deposits will be wiped out in a bank failure. That, among other reasons, is why we need publicly provided accounts where households and businesses can hold their money, risk-free'.[6]

Financial instability manifested itself on the other side of the pond, too. Credit Suisse, one of Europe's largest banks, also found itself in trouble after the collapse of the US banks. Dark clouds had been hanging over the bank for two years. It was an open secret. The bank lost money and prestige with foolhardy investments in leveraged funds, a frenzied bonus culture and a CEO who hired private investigators to spy on his management. It kept making headlines for all the wrong reasons. When one of the main investors, a Saudi oil tycoon, decided to withdraw from the bank, the floodgates opened. Up to 10 billion Swiss francs were being withdrawn daily, and the bank collapsed. The Swiss state intervened with an emergency loan of fifty billion Swiss francs. It negotiated a takeover by UBS, Credit Suisse's arch-rival, for the bargain price of three billion, with an additional guarantee for short-term loans of 150 billion Swiss francs.

'No more bank bailouts!', people said after the 2008 crisis. Fifteen years later, Silicon Valley Bank and Credit Suisse show that, even today, the big banks are too big to fail. In other words, the government, and by extension, the taxpayer, are still on the hook for speculators' reckless behaviour. When things go well, the profits flow to the private sector; when things go badly, the losses are nationalized. This was the case in the capitalism of 2008. This is still the case in the capitalist world of 2023.

6 Gerald Epstein, 'The Financial Crisis of 2023: Protecting Big Finance, Coming and Going', Institute for New Economic Thinking, Ineteconomics. org, 7 March 2023.

BlackRock and Co.

The 2008 banking crisis had countless losers and very few winners. Some winners remained in the shadows. One of them is the US-based BlackRock. In 2009, after acquiring the asset management division of British bank Barclays, the company quietly crowned itself the world's largest asset manager. Yes, BlackRock had its ducks in a row.

For BlackRock is not a bank, but an 'asset manager': a euphemism for 'money collector' or 'big speculator'. Asset managers invest on behalf of others, primarily institutional investors such as pension funds and insurance companies. Historically, these funds did the investing themselves; today, they increasingly outsource this task to specialised asset managers that charge fees for their services.

Asset managers are not subject to banking regulations, which were tightened in the aftermath of the 2008 financial crisis. So, a firm like BlackRock has no bank branches, no teller counters, and no public interaction with clients. It collects money from large investors and uses it to buy financial and other assets. BlackRock is part of what has come to be known as the 'shadow banking' sector: financial institutions that act like banks but aren't banks. A report by the Global Financial Stability Board estimates that the non-bank financial institutions, as these shadow banks are formally known, manage more than $240,000 billion.[1] That equates to almost half of all financial products in the world. The shadow is almost as big as the sun.

The unregulated world of shadow banking produces what unregulated worlds always produce: junk. The trade-in subprime

1 Financial Stability Board, 'Global Monitoring Report on Non-Bank Financial Intermediation 2022', 20 December 2022.

corporate debt, junk loans from zombie companies, has thus exploded into a market of more than five trillion dollars. Junk loans are repackaged as collateralised loan obligations, financial products that offer a handsome return in times of low-interest rates. But they are opaque and barely regulated. And junk ultimately remains junk. It all reeks of 2008, the pungent smell of crisis.

Asset management's big three, BlackRock, Vanguard, and State Street Global Advisors, have huge amounts of money to invest. They put it into financial assets like stocks or bonds, hoping for investment gains. It has created a massive concentration of ownership and power among a handful of elites. The Big Three own shares in just about every major publicly traded company, whether listed on the S&P 500 on Wall Street, the FTSE 350 in London, the DAX 30 in Frankfurt, the CAC 40 in Paris, or the BEL 20 in Brussels. For example, BlackRock holds voting rights in more than 17,000 companies in virtually every sector and country.

The German Institute for Economic Research is raising the alarm. It warns of the growing dominance of 'US asset managers' in the ownership structures of listed companies in Germany, especially as this has led to these funds 'increasingly co-owning German companies'.[2] US capital is increasingly buying into German and other companies: that's not soft power but hard power; it's all about ownership.

In the 1980s, asset managers began diversifying their holdings into 'real assets'. Rather than investing in financial assets, they started buying physical things, especially housing and infrastructure. As a result, more and more apartment buildings, offices, shopping malls and student housing are finding their way into the hands of asset managers, along with water mains, bridges, power grids, roads, and hospitals. Today, asset managers target revenue streams from wind farms, parking garages, buses, homes, hotels, and data centres.

2 DIW Berlin, 'US-Vermögensverwalter zunehmend als gemeinsame Eigentümer in deutschen Unternehmen vertreten', Diw.de, 9 August 2023.

Australia's Macquarie, for example, owns infrastructure that 100 million people depend on daily. Asset managers collectively own more than four trillion dollars' worth of housing and infrastructure.[3] That's a large-scale takeover of government, brazenly called 'privatisation'. And so, the basic pillars of a modern society fall into the hands of speculators. Because, let's be clear, asset managers are not long-term investors; they are everyday speculators who buy cheaply to resell at the highest possible price within five years or so. Asset managers and governments are worlds apart. As Australian journalist Gideon Haigh once remarked: 'An [asset manager] undertaking roles previously performed by the government is anything but a like-for-like swap. A government is elected on the basis of what it may giveth; an [asset manager] is chiefly interested in what it can taketh away'.[4]

High time for a return to public ownership.

3 'Our Lives in Their Portfolios — owners in the shadows', *Financial Times*, 30 May 2023.
4 Brett Christophers, 'Our new financial masters. How asset managers work in the shadows – and shape all of our lives', *The New Statesman*, 27 April 2023.

Austerity 2.0

Those who do not move, do not notice their chains.
   Rosa Luxemburg

'Escape route'. This word reminds me of *Prison Break*, the TV show about an engineer who gets locked up in a maximum-security prison to help his brother escape. He had the escape route tattooed in code on his body.

The European Commission also has an 'escape route'. But it's not in a code or a tattoo. It's in a clause. It's the escape route from the coercive Stability and Growth Pact. European 'economic governance' is based on this pact: strict, coercive budget and debt standards that the EU imposes on its member states.

On 11 March 2020, the World Health Organisation declared COVID-19 a pandemic. Nine days later, the European Commission decided to activate its escape clause. That sounds intriguing, and it is. For years, the Commission has insisted that it is unrealistic, even impossible, to deviate from the budget and debt standards. These standards can be summed up in two strict numbers from the Maastricht Treaty.

But what is the Maastricht Treaty? In February 1992, in preparation for the introduction of the single currency, the euro, the member states of Europe agreed in Maastricht that a country should not have more debt than it produces in wealth each year. Public debt must be kept below 60 per cent of GDP. And the national budgetary deficit – what a country's government spends and takes in each year – may not exceed 3per cent. These sacred numbers – sixty and three – are as arbitrary as they come. They have led to severe cuts, with the government restricting spending everywhere possible: sectors were privatised, public investment was reduced, and social services were phased out. All to meet the 'Maastricht standards'.

But in March 2020, the 60 per cent and 3 per cent were put on hold. The strict rules were suspended for a while. There was no other way because the pandemic lockdowns had basically shut down the entire economy. European member states reached deep into their pockets, each in their own way, to prop up health sectors or large private corporations, which would have been impossible under the pact's strict fiscal rules. Initially, the Commission limited the suspension of the rules to one year. But that proved a bit too optimistic. The Stability and Growth Pact remained on hold in 2022 and 2023.

What would happen if the rules of the Pact were reintroduced in the four largest eurozone economies: France, Italy, Germany, and Spain? The German Hans Böckler Foundation examined that question. The foundation published the results in September 2022. Reinstating the strict rules without any change would lead to an unprecedented reduction in government spending. In Italy, for example, it would be a one-fifth reduction. It's immediately obvious: this cannot happen.

The German government, which was the most insistent on reinstating strict standards, then came up with a compromise. Looking at how government spending compares to growth projections, it wanted to allow a little more flexibility. The Hans Böckler Foundation knew that even this suggestion was not very helpful. Under this scenario, Italy would still have to continuously cut 15 per cent of its public spending. The macroeconomic consequences would also be enormous. The cost-cutting burden would reduce annual growth in the eurozone to a meagre 1.2 per cent. Such an approach would be a recipe for social revolt, the German research institute warned.

~~~

The temporary suspension of the debt and budget rules expired at the end of 2023. The European Commission and European governments are in total agreement: the standards will continue to be reinstated as long as they are necessary.

In November 2022, the European Commission released the first balloons for this purpose. The arbitrary targets of no more than 60 per cent public debt and no more than a 3 per cent budgetary deficit remain the starting point. However, the Commission wants to change the approach to prevent member states like Italy from going completely off the deep end and dragging the entire eurozone down with them. In exchange for liberal reforms, member states would be able to postpone certain cuts through individual agreements with the Commission.

With this approach, the focus is now on analysing the sustainability of a member state's public debt. In European jargon, it is the debt sustainability assessment or DSA for short. Previously, all member states had to meet the same quantitative targets at all costs. This turned out to be impossible because the situation differs too much from country to country. So now they're going to fine-tune and adjust the imposed 'reforms' country by country. Each member state will have to constantly consult with the Commission and convince it that it is truly committed to implementing the agreed cuts.

The Commission found the model for this approach at the International Monetary Fund and the World Bank. The DSA model has been in vogue there for many years. Will a country experience strong growth in the future? Will interest rates remain under control? A higher level of debt is not such a problem in that case. The answers to these questions about the future are just assumptions. It's certainly not an exact science. Yet, how much a country will have to save on its hospitals, schools, or public services depends on these DSA estimates. And criteria such as employment, wages, poverty, and social exclusion are completely disregarded in the assessment, notes the European Trade Union Confederation.

While DSA may sound like a technical matter, it's anything but. After all, the European Commission will also include an assessment of the policies pursued in the member states in the sustainability analysis. For example, a member state's progressive and social investment policy may come up against a DSA veto. If the Commission finds that a member state's public debt is sustainable, that member state will be able to borrow money on the financial markets with relative ease. But what if the Commission takes a negative view of a public debt? You can bet your bottom dollar that the rating agencies will also pick up on it and downgrade the country's credit rating. Then, borrowing becomes much more expensive because of higher interest rates. And you get a snowball effect leading to the abyss. Professor Paul De Grauwe calls it the self-fulfilling prophecies of the European governance model.

Berlin's Bullies

'A lot of people thought that just because Germany now had a social democratic chancellor and the Greens were in government, it would give up its commitment to stable public finances and pursue other ideas', said Christian Lindner, the liberal minister of finance and the new face of Germany's tough economic line. 'But that's not the case'.[1]

Greater flexibility in European austerity policy is out of the question for Lindner. He takes up his pen for an op-ed in *Die Welt*. To lend weight to his message, he persuades the finance ministers of the Czech Republic, Austria, Bulgaria, Denmark, Croatia, Slovenia, Lithuania, Latvia, Estonia, and Luxembourg to co-sign it. It's no coincidence that these are countries with close economic and commercial ties to Germany and that may not have or want the balance of power to antagonize German big guns. Lindner doesn't like the fact that countries can negotiate their DSAs with the Commission individually. He wants Germany to be able to watch over other countries preparing their budgets. Multilateral surveillance is what he calls it. He also wants 'quantitative criteria that apply to all member states', with 'clear minimum requirements'. Lindner believes that highly indebted countries should reduce their debt by 1 per cent of gross domestic product each year. A linear measure that applies to all.

'The greatest threat to European democracy is inappropriate and mistimed fiscal discipline forced down the throats of a majority of Europe's voters by a minority coalition of "northern" states. It would be disastrous if Germany were to put itself at the

---

1 Guy Chazan and Sam Fleming, 'Germany warns of stalemate on EU fiscal rules reform', *Financial Times*, 9 June 2023.

head of that coalition', economist Joseph Stiglitz warned.[2] New cuts will cause further impoverishment and create fertile ground for the rise of the far right. 'For the electoral chances of the nationalist populists in Italy, there would be nothing better than the prospect of a confrontation with the German Finance Ministry. That would be disastrous for Italy. It would be bad for Europe. And it would be bad for Germany', said Stiglitz.

~~~

On 26 April 2023, the European Commission presented two regulations and a directive to shape the new European austerity policy. The sacred numbers of 3 per cent and 60 per cent remain the cornerstones of the policy. The *Fiscal Compact* also remains in force. That was the foundation of the tough austerity policy that started in 2012.

Anyone under the illusion that progressive reform was imminent was in for an unpleasant surprise. For those who do not meet the austerity targets, the enforcement of rules and standards will become even stricter. Member states must submit annual progress reports. This allows the Commission to monitor and enforce compliance with the savings commitments more effectively. Member states with high public debt will automatically be subject to a correction procedure with sanctions if they deviate from the agreed fiscal adjustment path.

That's a long-winded way of saying Berlin is essentially getting its way. And not concerning linear debt reduction but concerning linear deficit reduction. The same standards and numbers apply to all countries precisely as Lindner had pushed for. If a member state's budget deficit exceeds 3 per cent of its gross domestic product, a mandatory minimum saving of 0.5 per cent of GDP per year is imposed. These may seem like minor figures, but they aren't.

---

2 Joseph E. Stiglitz and Adam Tooze, 'Es wäre ein Fehler, ihm seinen Wunsch zu erfüllen', *Die Zeit*, 27 October 2021.

The European Trade Union Confederation (ETUC) calculated that these figures would mean spending cuts of at least 45 billion euros for 14 European countries in 2024.[3]

~~~

The EU is not in good shape. In the summer of 2023, the eurozone entered a mild recession: the economy contracted by 0.1 per cent for two quarters in a row. The continent seems on the verge of irrelevance due to the growing rivalry between the United States and China. The US is trying to pull European industry across the pond with all kinds of protectionist measures. We'll cover that topic in the next chapter.

The EU urgently needs an industrial plan with public investment in energy, transportation, fibre optic networks, housing, and infrastructure. These aren't ordinary expenses you can delete or postpone; they determine the future. But budget rules put a stop to this. The new austerity obsession will also torpedo the EU's climate ambitions. Europe aims to be carbon neutral by 2050 and halve net greenhouse gas emissions by 2030. This requires investment in renewable energy, sustainable mobility, and the renovation and insulation of homes and buildings. The estimated additional annual investment requirement is in the order of €430 billion.[4] Under the new rules, this is impossible.

Social investment in education, healthcare, and social security systems is also coming under severe pressure. The healthcare sector is creaking across the EU. Larger budgets are needed everywhere, in care for the elderly, childcare, you name it. The same is true for education. Yet the EU wants to save €45 billion in 2024. You could use that to pay for a million nurses, or 1.5 million

---

3 ETUC, EU Rules Require €45 Billion In Spending Cuts Next Year, 24 May 2023.

4 Luc Triangle, 'Austerity ahead? EU fiscal rules must encourage investment, not hamper the twin transition', *IndustriAll Europe*, 4 April 2023.

teachers. Belgium is expected to save €2.7 billion in EU funding in 2024. That's equivalent to nearly forty thousand nurses or eighty thousand teachers.[5]

Despite the Commission's plans, reality tells us that gigantic investments are, in fact, needed. And not with big business in charge. Because we've already had that in the years of free money after the banking crisis and during the pandemic. A lot of money was lent to big businesses, almost for free, but it did not flow into productive investments. Now, it's up to the government to take the initiative. It needs a public investment plan in energy, transportation, housing, healthcare, and digitalisation. I've called it a Prometheus plan. Ten young talents have worked it out under the name *Doe de Switch!* (Make the Switch!).[6]

European treaties are a barrier to the return of public monopolies. These treaties must go. We need a strong European Investment Fund, and public investment by member states should be kept out of the budget balance. Today, the opposite is true. Germany is imposing its rules. We are heading for a new wave of austerity measures.

Meanwhile, more public money is going to military spending. NATO requires member states to spend at least 2 per cent of their gross domestic product on defence each year. Expansion plans for the European military-industrial complex are on the table. So, Europe is caught between the hammer and the anvil, between mindless cuts and military spending. And all at the expense of education, healthcare, housing, transportation, and the climate.

We seem doomed to repeat the euro crisis of 2011. But more so now, in a time of war, social unrest, and polarisation.

The European Trade Union Confederation launched the

5 ETUC, EU Rules Require €45 Billion In Spending Cuts Next Year, 24 May 2023.

6 Peter Mertens, *Ze zijn ons vergeten De werkende klasse, de zorg en de crisis die komt*, Berchem: EPO, 2020, p.126. Also see Raoul Hedebouw, *Doe de switch*, EPO, Berchem, 2022.

'Stop Austerity 2.0' campaign with a petition, actions, and demonstrations to oppose the austerity plans and the new EU rules. If the Commission pushes its way through, it can expect a strong reaction from across the continent.

Chapter 3

From Energy Revolution to Trade War

Liam

I have this one little saying,
when things get too heavy
just call me helium,
the lightest known gas to man.
  Jimi Hendrix

In Ludwigshafen, the Rhine's meanders once created a wide, swampy floodplain that would be waterlogged in winter. When the Rhine was straightened in the 1820s, a drop in the groundwater level made room for a new city directly on the banks of the Rhine. The city centre sits on a plateau of filled-in streets. The courtyards are still at the old lowland level, adding an extra floor to the backs of many houses. Friedrich Engelhorn moved his chemical company BASF (Baden Aniline & Soda Factory) to this new city. BASF specialized in synthetic dyes, developing alizarin red and indigo. The company rapidly expanded, and Ludwigshafen became a chemical city.

Today, Ludwigshafen is one of the wealthiest industrial cities in Germany. At night, the Rhine reflects the thousands of lights from the chemical plants for kilometres. The chemical lights are easily mistaken for stars burning in the water. BASF Ludwigshafen is an integrated chemical complex covering an area of ten square kilometres – the largest in the world. A city within the city. Three thousand kilometres of pipelines and two hundred kilometres of railways connect two hundred production sites.

Liam, a youthful forty-something with a lively beard, has worked there for years as a process operator on the ammonia production line. I got to know him through some German friends.

According to the media, a disaster is imminent in Ludwigshafen because gas is terribly expensive. I contact Liam. Liam's voice is clear, despite our poor video connection. 'I spent eight years training to be a process operator here, which is longer than a doctor', he laughs. 'You have to learn about the whole plant step by step, you have to learn how to draw it, and only then are you trained to be able to control the plant'.

How hard are things there? I ask him.

'We shut down tomorrow, Peter. Gas has become way too expensive. We can produce eight hundred thousand tonnes of ammonia a year here, but everything is at a standstill now'. He struggles to continue.

What does gas have to do with ammonia?, I prompt him, awkwardly.

'Without ammonia, there's no manure, Peter. And without manure, there's no food. Natural gas is needed to produce ammonia. The pipes run directly from our natural gas cracker to our colleagues in ammonia production for further processing. But this gas has become so expensive that they are better off buying ammonia abroad'.

Liam later told me that the cracker had not been used since he had shut it down. 'They did keep us busy though'. He begins to count on his fingers all the little chores and training sessions he has done. 'They even made us use the simulator to create virtual ammonia because they were afraid we'd forget what to do when we were up and running again'. He lost a lot of sleep worrying about the gloomy forecasts, to no avail. In March 2023, management closed the cracker for good. Hundreds of jobs were on the line.

~ ~ ~

BASF runs on gas: for energy and as a feedstock. For years, it had been able to count on cheap gas from Russia. However, the war and sanctions forced German industry to cancel its long-term gas contracts. It had to look for alternatives in the expensive spot market. Although gas prices have peaked, BASF expects energy costs to remain three times higher than before.[1]

The gas fields in the European Union barely cover a tenth of European consumption. So, the EU depends on foreign countries. And for half a century, Russia met this demand with pipelines supplying gas storage facilities in Germany and elsewhere directly from Siberian gas fields, providing almost half of the continent's consumption. With the war, that gas went out of the window, leaving Europe rushing to find a replacement, which is no easy task. A pipeline is not a garden shed; it's not something you build over a sunny weekend.

This sudden shift in European gas supply presents a unique opportunity for the United States, requiring presidential action to capitalise on it. Joe Biden closes his lucrative gas deal a month after the Russian invasion of Ukraine. Europe is switching to liquefied gas, some of which comes from the US. When natural gas is cooled down to -162°C, an energy-consuming process, it becomes *liquefied*. And that's where the name Liquefied Natural Gas or LNG comes from. You don't need a pipeline; you can transport it across the ocean in big gas tankers. A large proportion of LNG from the United States is shale gas. High-pressure pumping of a bevvy of chemicals deep into the ground to extract gas from shale: that's *fracking*, and it's incredibly harmful. Shale gas is ten times more harmful to the climate than normal gas. Massive amounts of methane, a potent greenhouse gas, are released during fracking. When you add up all the effects, liquefied shale gas is as bad for the climate as coal.[2]

'Pushing new toxic export facilities and decades more methane gas is a death sentence for those on the frontlines of the climate emergency', said Kassie Siegel, director of the Centre for Biological

1 Madeleine Bruder, 'BASF/Russia: Ending Faustian Pact Creates Recurring Costs for Germany', *Financial Times*, 18 January 2023.
2 Raphaël Schmeller, 'Vollgas für Fracking', *Junge Welt*, 15 June 2022.

Diversity's Climate Law Institute[3] US gas companies have been struggling to sell their expensive shale gas for a long time. More than half of their plants were idle as recently as 2016. But the war and sanctions against Russia have changed everything.

~~~

In the first nine months of 2022, Europe's imports of US shale gas are worth €35 billion, four times more than the previous year.[4] For the next few years, the EU will inevitably run on dirty gas, which is also extremely expensive. Prices are soaring because everyone wants to import it. A scarcity mindset is ideal for boosting speculation. And gas dealers know it. Asia-bound tankers do an about-turn and head for Europe. It pays better. By November 2022, a tenth of the world's gas tanker fleet will be plying Europe's waters. 'Ships seek to maximise the return on their combined $2 billion cargo', writes the *Financial Times*.[5] The traders are idling their massive vessels off Europe's coast as they hold out for higher prices.

With ship-based LNG supplies so high, expensive onshore offloading facilities, such as those in Zeebrugge and Spain, are rapidly being built. It's like a Santiago de Compostela of gas. The gas lobby pushes for three hundred new gas terminals in Europe.[6] We're talking about billions in investment, which will undoubtedly be reflected in our gas bills in the coming years. Incidentally, the gas switch doesn't mean an end to the flow of Russian gas to

3 Oliver Milman, 'US plan to provide 15 bn cubic meters of natural gas to EU alarms climate groups', *The Guardian*, 25 March 2022.
4 Gavin Maguire, 'Column-U.S. LNG exports both a lifeline and a drain for Europe in 2023', *Reuters*, 21 December 2022.
5 Shotaro Tani, 'LNG tankers idle off Europe's coast as traders wait for gas price rise', *Financial Times*, 3 November 2022.
6 Corporate Europe Observatory, 'Fuelling the cost of living crisis. How the fossil fuel industry turned the Ukraine war into an opportunity for extra profits and further lock-in of gas', Corporateeurope.org, 28 October 2022.

Europe. The additional supplies promised from the United States are far from enough to replace Russian gas. The tap has not been switched off completely.

Since the Nord Stream pipeline sabotage, a limited amount of Russian gas is still arriving by land, either through the Ukraine pipeline or the TurkStream pipeline. If the deal to transport Russian gas through Ukraine is not renewed, 'we'll soon risk having to reduce or even shut down our industrial production', warned the German Minister of Energy, Robert Habeck, in June 2023.[7]

One thing's for sure: US President Biden's gas deal is a golden one. He's tying the big European market to US shale gas, something his predecessors never managed to do. Biden said such a step was not only 'the right thing to do from a moral standpoint', but it was 'going to put us on a stronger strategic footing'. [8] He's right about that. The gas deal is the first strategic battle in this time of war: very expensive liquefied gas weakens the position of European industry in favour of the US industry.

The industrial heart of Europe, Germany, is where the energy switch hits particularly hard. Industrial production has declined there, particularly in the energy-intensive sectors: the chemical industry and metal processing. Private consumption has also fallen, mainly due to high energy and food prices. Germany has entered a recession. Unlike previous downturns, no politicians or economists are rushing to explain that this is just a blip and the big upturn is just around the corner.

Liam doesn't yet know whether he'll be able to continue working in other areas of the plant. The uncertainty is gnawing at him: 'I feel like a yo-yo: up and down, up and down. I've no idea what will happen to my job'.

---

7 OWF, Ostdeutsches Wirtschaftsforum, Rede von Robert Habeck, 12 June 2023.

8 Rob Davies, 'Biden and EU agree landmark gas deal to break Kremlin's hold', *The Guardian*, 25 March 2022.

The White Bellbird

The Amazon rainforest is a deafeningly noisy place, a constant cacophony of jungle animals trying to make themselves heard. Amid the din, the male white bellbird has evolved a winning strategy – he may be the loudest bird on Earth.
    National Geographic, October 2019

Alexander De Croo, Belgium's liberal prime minister, is disgruntled. 'The US, our partner...they call our industry. And they tell them why are you investing in Europe? You should come over to the US'. The prime minister continues: 'Calling German firms and Belgian firms in a very aggressive way – don't invest in Europe, we have something better...I think they were very well aware of the impact that it could have'.[1] De Croo knows Europe's economy is in bad shape. The challenges are putting pressure on everything. He is sad to see the United States trying to lure European companies across the pond with lots of lip service and subsidies.

High energy prices are primarily a European issue. And producing on the old continent has become a lot more expensive. Many countries have reduced production in recent months. The handbrake is on everywhere: in steel, paper, ceramics, glass, fertilisers, and cars.[2] How do we keep strategic investments here? It is a crucial question for Europe to answer in the race of the twenty-first century. Companies are not only looking at the costs,

---

1 Andy Bounds, 'Belgium accuses US of "aggressive" push to lure European business', *Financial Times*, 10 January 2023.
2 Guy Chazan and Patricia Nilsson, 'Germany confronts a broken business model', *Financial Times*, 6 December 2022.

but also at their chances of receiving subsidies. Investment is a costly and risky business. And big business is only too happy to count on government support.

The first day of 2023 was a tipping point.

The US government launched a huge subsidy programme: the Inflation Reduction Act. It's opening its money belt and unleashing a $369 billion mountain of subsidies to support companies that want to manufacture in the United States. With a subsidy pot like that, you can already start calling the Belgian or German industry. It has put De Croo and his European colleagues on edge. The US plans to target strategic sectors of the future: car batteries, wind turbines, solar cells, semiconductors. You can count on generous subsidies if you produce the technology of the future for Uncle Sam.

Faced with such a tempting offer, some European industries start wavering. Europe's largest battery manufacturer, Sweden's Northvolt, had planned to invest in Germany until a call came from across the pond. You can get $600 to $800 million support from us in the US for your new plant, said the voice at the other end.[3] Northvolt hesitated. After much deliberation, the company finally decided to build a new plant in Heiden, Germany. The plant will produce batteries for one million cars a year. So, what convinced the Swedes? The answer is simple: €600 million in German government subsidies.[4]

Europe's largest industrial solar cell producer, Meyer Burger, did exactly the same thing. In a letter to the German minister of finance, the company openly threatened to cancel its investment programme in the Federal Republic of Germany and to look across the ocean for new projects. On the public broadcaster ZDF, CEO Gunter Erfurt explains to viewers how it works: 'For one gigawatt

3 Sam Fleming, Andy Bounds, Richard Milne, Sarah White, Guy Chazan, and Barney Jopson, 'European industry pivots to US as Biden subsidy sends "dangerous signal"', *Financial Times*, 19 November 2022.

4 Supantha Mukherjee and Victoria Waldersee, 'Europe set for two new gigafactories as it lures battery makers', *Reuters*, 13 May 2023.

of solar cells and solar modules, you can get $110 million a year in the United States until 2029!'.[5] A stark message to the German government: if there are no subsidies, we're out of here. It's the dawn of a subsidy war.

At first, not everyone is happy about that. 'There has been a mutinous mood among some American allies in both Europe and Asia at the scale of the new US subsidies', reports the *Financial Times* in July 2023.[6] A mutinous mood indeed. But this European mutiny turns out not to be so serious after all. Here and there, a European official calls for a big fuss to be made at the World Trade Organisation about the subsidy war, and German vice chancellor Robert Habeck mumbles words to the effect of 'it's like a declaration of war'. But it's not long before the Europeans fall back meekly into a willing Atlantic fold.

~~~

Biologists say the white bellbird has the loudest call in the world. The females choose the male with the loudest call to be their mate. The world of business is similar. The blaring US subsidy lure is working. Italy's Enel is to build a new solar panel plant in Oklahoma with the help of $280 million in subsidies and tax credits.[7] Germany's Siemens is entering the US market to build a smart energy grid.[8] And France's Air Liquide will produce heavily subsidised green hydrogen there.[9] The white bellbird sings triumphantly.

5 Ralf Wurzbacher, 'Subventionswettlauf, Europa verzockt Zukunft', *junge Welt*, 15 June 2023.

6 Guy Chazan, Sam Fleming and Kana Inagaki, 'A global subsidy war? Keeping up with the Americans', *Financial Times*, 13 July 2023.

7 Nichola Groom, 'Italy's Enel to invest more than $1 bln in Oklahoma solar panel factory', *Reuters*, 22 May 2023.

8 Christoph Steitz, 'Siemens Energy plans U.S. power grids push to tap into IRA boost', *Reuters*, 25 May 2023.

9 Andrey Sychev and Bartosz Dabrowski, 'Air Liquide sees historic opportunity to invest in clean energy', *Reuters*, 16 February 2023.

Meanwhile, in Berlin, industry leaders are at a loss for words. A survey by BDI, the Federation of German Industries, shows that one in six companies is actively moving parts of its production and jobs abroad. Another 30 per cent of medium-sized companies are considering doing the same.[10] 'Almost two-thirds of the companies we interviewed consider prices of energy and resources to be among the most pressing challenges', said BDI President Siegfried Russwurm. 'For further investment, industries in Germany require slashing of red tape and targeted tax cuts'.[11]

Meanwhile, by far the most powerful lobby group of European large-scale industry, the European Round Table for Industry, has started hammering on the same nail: more subsidies with fewer conditions! State aid rules should be relaxed, the lobby argues.[12] Step by step, the lines are moving. For years, *Industriepolitik* was a dirty word in Germany. When East Germans asked for a new industrial policy after the dismantling of their own industry, the silence was deafening. For Germany's ordo-liberals, the orthodox hardliners who oppose state intervention, the mere suggestion of an industrial policy was an insult. But today, liberal textbooks must yield to geostrategic interests. Now, only Industriepolitik is on the agenda in Berlin. This brings Germany into line with France's more interventionist industrial policy. From now on, it's opening the purse strings to give big companies like ThyssenKrupp huge sums of money.

By relaxing European state aid rules, the EU wanted to compete with the subsidy blitz from Washington. However, the fact that individual EU member states can grant this state aid is also causing resentment because they are not all sitting on a hoard

10 Handelsblatt, 'Deutsche Industriebetriebe verlagern Jobs und Produktion ins Ausland', 7 June 2023.

11 Nick Alipour, 'German economy at risk as companies plan to leave country', *Euractiv*, 6 June 2023.

12 Sam Fleming, Andy Bounds, Richard Milne, Sarah White, Guy Chazan, and Barney Jopson, 'European industry pivots to US as Biden subsidy sends "dangerous signal"', *Financial Times*, 19 November 2022.

of capital to support their own industries. 'There is the danger of a two-speed EU emerging. The lack of a common monetary fund for all EU states means that investments will be made by the large states that have room for budgetary manoeuvres, primarily Germany and France. (...) of the danger of creating harmful competition between EU member states'.[13]

In the spring of 2023, the European Commission launched two proposals: the *Net-Zero Industry Act* and the *Critical Raw Materials Act*. The Net-Zero Industry Act seeks to expand the production capacity of private companies with net-zero technologies that reduce emissions to zero. Large subsidies have been released for that purpose. The Critical Raw Materials Act should make it easier to license the mining of rare raw materials in Europe, including lithium and cobalt, for wind turbines, batteries, and solar panels. The legislation is controversial: mining these metals will cause considerable environmental damage. According to the World Wildlife Fund, such a green transition comes at the expense of nature and biodiversity.

The two legislative bills have failed to convince the industry. The captains of industry use damning statements – and a move across the ocean as leverage – to drive up the price. 'I need simplicity. The US has adopted a simple strategy that immediately incentivises businesses to invest while the EU is coming with a political framework that lacks precise elements and misses simple, clear-cut reasons for businesses to invest', complains Ilham Kadri, CEO of Belgium chemicals company Solvay.[14] It's a race to pile support on large private companies to cover their investment risks.

'This state-capital relationship involves lots of carrots for the private sector, in the form of grants and tax credits that will boost corporate profits and companies' market shares, with almost no

13 'Spectre of a two-speed EU returns', *Revista*, 7 February 2023.
14 Peggy Hollinger, Cheng Ting-Fang and Andy Bounds, 'EU industrialists attack Europe's counter to Biden green bonanza', *Financial Times*, 20 March 2023.

sticks', explains economist Daniella Gabor.[15] The government helps big businesses with their returns on investment but sets hardly any requirements when it comes to the returns for society, which flows back to society. Socialise the risks, privatise the profits – this earworm has been buzzing in my head all morning.

As disgruntled as De Croo may be, Washington doesn't lose sleep over the murmurs of a Belgian prime minister. Ultimately, the focus of the huge US subsidy programmes lies elsewhere: its rivalry with Asia and, more specifically, with China.

15 Mehreen Khan, 'Putting power in private hands for clean energy race stores up trouble', *The Sunday Times*, 23 May 2023.

One the Industry,

the Other the Banks?

Instead of citizens, it produces consumers. Instead of communities, it produces shopping malls. The net result is an atomised society of disengaged individuals who feel demoralised and socially powerless. In sum, neoliberalism is the immediate and foremost enemy of genuine participatory democracy.

Noam Chomsky

In the late nineteenth century, the US activist Elizabeth Magie was deep in thought. Magie was at home in rural Illinois. A place where few had much, and many had to make do with little. How could she make it clear that landowners shouldn't be allowed to grab land and homes? The young feminist believed that the world belongs to everyone. Magie wanted to reach many people, not just those who read books. And then she had a light-bulb moment: a board game. Everyone plays those!

Magie created a board game, *The Landlord's Game*, the first with a circuit. She applied for a patent. For Magie, the game's purpose was clear: demonstrating the dangers of monopolised land ownership. She said, 'In a short time, I hope a very short time, men and women will discover that they are poor because Carnegie and Rockefeller have more than they know what to do with'. Steel baron Carnegie and oil magnate Rockefeller, the United States' first billionaire, symbolised the growing monopoly ownership of the time. You could play the game in two ways: as a monopolist and as an anti-monopolist. In the monopoly version, the goal is to crush your opponents and wipe them off the board. In the anti-monopoly version, the game ends when the player who started with the least amount of money has doubled his capital.

The Landlord's Game was a hit. The toy manufacturer Parker Brothers bought the patent in 1935. The game got a new look and a new name: *Monopoly*. From then on, there was only one rule: the triumph of one over all. For decades, *Monopoly* was the toy manufacturer's cash cow. The board game came to symbolise capitalist greed. Today, hardly anyone is aware that Elizabeth Magie once designed her parlour game as a stinging indictment of the system: left to their own devices, markets will soon lead to monopolies with virtually unchallengeable power.

~~~

What was an indictment in *The Landlord's Game* is now the norm. The doctrine of a completely free market, independent of state intervention, reducing articulate citizens to consumers and democracy to share ownership. Inequality as a virtue, and wealth is an indicator. All these ideas pass themselves off as biological laws, something you cannot avoid, like the air we breathe. More and more people have internalised the doctrine. The rich convince themselves that they have earned their wealth, and the poor begin to blame themselves for their failures, even though their living conditions are not their fault.

Neoliberalism, which only really took off in the 1970s, when the economy was in decline, took this belief system to new heights. The prescriptive approach also gained traction with Margaret Thatcher and Ronald Reagan at the helm. The doctrine became a reality: huge tax cuts for the rich, deregulation, freeing up financial markets, privatisation, and opening up world trade through institutions like the International Monetary Fund and the World Trade Organisation.

If Elizabeth Magie were alive, she would immediately design

a new board game based on so much free trade, but it would have a global circuit.

~~~

Neoliberal policies have dramatically changed the economic landscape. The United States accounted for half of world production until well into the 1960s. In the northwest Manufacturing Belt, the world's steel was cast, and cars rolled off the assembly line at the pace of a heartbeat. The United States was the factory of the world, and the centre of global consumption and financial activity. That rapidly changed. US capital began travelling the world in search of places where it could produce at a low cost – for the US market, of course. Production was moved to what was simplistically referred to as 'low-wage countries'. What remained? Financial institutions. As controls and regulations were phased out, they yielded more and more returns. Companies were listed on the stock exchange, and shareholder returns became the be-all and end-all of corporate management.

Free from government intervention, US capital roamed the world in search of countries that could provide the raw materials: countries such as Russia and Brazil. But it also looked for countries that processed the raw materials into new products, countries such as Turkey and China, which tentatively opened their markets to foreign capital in the late 1970s. Raw materials, imposed monoculture, finished products: the rest of the world was plundered, all to serve consumption in the West.

Manufacturing systematically moved away from the United States. Those in power didn't mind. With its technological superiority and the dollar as the world currency, Washington was assured of control. And then there was the crushing military might of the Pentagon and its overseas bases, should some stray progressive government get it into its head to nationalise a company and use the country's wealth for its own development.

In 1954, the United States overthrew the democratically elected president of Guatemala, Jacobo Árbenz, because he had dared to challenge the power of the United Fruit Company with his land reforms. It was a prelude, for impunity rewards the crime, encourages its repetition, and allows it to propagate. For decades, Washington has been organising or supporting all kinds of regime change, without having to answer to anyone.

~~~

Freewheeling capital opened domestic markets and removed barriers and tariffs, with some beneficial but mostly damaging effects. Washington used the World Trade Organisation to impose its trade rules on all and sundry. More and more countries of the South became dependent on exporting their products to the West. They saw their prosperity tied to unstable global markets.

In late 2001, China joined the World Trade Organisation. Champagne corks popped at the White House. China, President Bill Clinton thought, would be pulled into the capitalist world system, and deal itself the final blow. So did his successor, George W. Bush. Washington thought it could outsmart Beijing by allowing China to join the World Trade Organisation. In China, WTO membership ensures the rapid development of new industries. Imports of raw materials and exports of manufactured goods grew rapidly. *Made in China* has become a household term. Cheap products from Asia allowed Americans to continue consuming in the United States, even though their wages barely rose.[1] And when US consumption fell at the end of the century, Washington made it much easier to borrow. Consuming on credit led to the banking crisis in 2008.

While the US economy became increasingly financially driven,

---

1 Lawrence Mishel, 'Growing inequalities, reflecting growing employer power, have generated a productivity-pay gap since 1979', Economic Policy Institute, 2 September 2021.

China was fully committed to industrialisation. Simply put, one became the world's bank, while the other became the world's manufacturer. It's almost like a division of labour.

Beijing's response to the 2008 global crisis was massive investment in infrastructure and manufacturing. To secure exports, the country built a new Silk Road. Step by step, the Chinese worked towards becoming the world export champion. Millions of Chinese moved from the countryside to the cities to work in the new factories. The economic boom was used to alleviate extreme poverty. Living standards rose rapidly. Meanwhile, China's focus was no longer on simple processes or intermediate products but on technology and high-end products. And not just for the global market, but increasingly for the home market of 1.3 billion people who had more and more money to spend.

Since 2000, China's investment in research and development has increased tenfold. It now spends $560 billion a year on it – only slightly less than the United States. The European Union is still dragging its feet with $380 billion. Not surprisingly, Chinese tech companies are working their way up. China has become a global economic factor and is making others nervous.

'In less than 50 years China has moved from widespread poverty and economic isolation to be the world's second-largest economy, and a leader in many cutting-edge technologies'. So says Ursula von der Leyen, president of the European Commission. 'Since 1978, growth has averaged over 9 per cent per year, and more than 800 million people were lifted out of poverty'.[2]

~~~

Clinton and Bush had hoped that admitting Beijing into the World Trade Organisation would allow them to pull the strings.

2 Ursula von der Leyen, 'Speech by President von der Leyen on EU-China relations to the Mercator Institute for China Studies and the European Policy Centre', European Commission, 30 March 2023.

But that gamble backfired on Washington. The world's industrial centre rapidly shifted to East Asia. Beijing became a leader in several future technologies: supercomputing, green energy, 6G telecommunications, aerospace, genetic engineering, and electric cars.[3]

So, in 2012, after years of parallel development between China and the United States, Washington had a change of strategy. That year, President Obama launched his Pivot to Asia strategy. US foreign policy no longer centred on the Middle East but on East Asia, especially China. In the United States, a new policy gradually emerged. Protectionism and state aid became high on the agenda. The Washington Consensus of the Chicago boys seemed to be dead and buried.

3 Jamie Gaida, Jenny Wong-Leung, Stephan Robin, and Danielle Cave, 'ASPI's Critical Technology Tracker - AUKUS updates', Australian Strategic Policy Institute, 2 March 2023.

Neoliberalism is Dead, is it Not?

When the winds of change blow,
some people build walls,
others build windmills.
     Chinese proverb

In May 2023, a Columbia University student got a tattoo on her upper arm for her graduation. The text leaves little to the imagination: *Death to neoliberalism.* Nothing to write home about, you might say. Every year, thousands of undergraduates reward themselves with a tattoo at the end of their studies. But it was a revelation for Rana Foroohar. She enthusiastically tweeted a photo of the tattoo into the Twittersphere. Foroohar is a global economic analyst for CNN and a regular columnist for the *Financial Times*. The 'death to neoliberalism' tattoo quickly took on a life of its own. Soon afterwards, Jennifer Harris, a long-serving senior voice in the Biden administration, shared the photograph.[1] Prominent figures from the US establishment declaring death to neoliberalism? It's a striking turn of events. The rise of China and Donald Trump's electoral success in the former Rust Belt are coming to a head: the United States has reached a turning point.

US national security advisor, Jake Sullivan, gave a speech at the prestigious Brookings Institution a few days before the student got her tattoo. Sullivan reflected on decades of neoliberal policies before a select gathering:

'When President Biden came into office more than two years

---

1 David Wallace-Wells, 'America's 'Neoliberal' Consensus Might Finally Be Dead', *The New York Times*, 25 May 2023.

ago, America's industrial base had been hollowed out. The vision of public investment that had energised the American project in the post-war years had faded. It had given way to a set of ideas that championed tax cutting and deregulation, privatisation over public action, and trade liberalisation as an end in itself.[2]

The security advisor doesn't mince his words:

'Now, no one – certainly not me – is discounting the power of markets. But in the name of oversimplified market efficiency, entire supply chains of strategic goods – along with the industries and jobs that made them – moved overseas.'[3]

Years of free-market policies and the outsourcing of jobs and production to low-wage countries have done more harm than good to America's position, Sullivan argues.

~~~

It's a remarkable turn of events. After all, hasn't the United States sworn a different ideological oath for decades? 'What's good for the markets is good for the United States, and what's good for the United States is good for the whole world', is how a generation of US leaders embraced capitalist globalisation and championed free trade. But below the rhetorical waterline, industry disappeared. Banks and hedge funds took over. According to Sullivan, that period is behind us. Trade deals should benefit people in Pennsylvania and Michigan, not Shenzhen and Shanghai. The United States triggered an industrial subsidy race by adopting the Inflation Reduction Act. The

2 Jake Sullivan, 'Remarks by National Security Advisor Jake Sullivan on Renewing American Economic Leadership at the Brookings Institution', Whitehouse.gov, 27 April 2023.
3 Ibid.

federal subsidies tap is open. So, too, is the doorway to protectionist measures: *Buy American*. Now that the neoliberal mantle has been cast aside, a new consensus is beginning to emerge. Gradually, market liberalism is giving way to state interventionism, and unlimited globalisation is giving way to the protection of domestic markets. Open markets and free trade are hardly mentioned by anyone across the whole US political spectrum.

Neoliberalism is dead, but perhaps less dead than the grand statements would suggest. The subsidies under the Inflation Reduction Act are a far cry from the major infrastructure programmes implemented by President Franklin Roosevelt to tackle the Great Depression of the 1930s. Roosevelt's New Deal was centred on public ownership. Although private companies completed many of the tens of thousands of construction projects, the government financed and owned almost all of the new infrastructure. Today, it is about subsidising and promoting private infrastructure, not about public works or public ownership. The focus is firmly on future-oriented sectors designed to have a multiplier effect on the rest of the economy, like a snowball rolling down a hill, getting bigger and bigger. The largest subsidies, such as Clean Electricity Investment and Clean Vehicle Tax Credit, only encourage private investment.

Predictably, the car industry's response to so much support has been enthusiastic. Thirty-six investment projects worth more than $40 billion have been announced. If you buy an electric vehicle in the United States, you can get $7,500 in tax credit. One condition is that its final assembly must be in North America, using North American battery components. No wonder countries with expertise in car manufacturing, such as Germany, are more than concerned about Washington's actions. The German Chamber of Commerce and Industry has labelled the subsidy a 'violation of world trade rules'.[4]

4 Ralf Wurzbacher, 'Subventionswettlauf, Europa verzockt Zukunft', *junge Welt*, 15 June 2023.

'As we move through the energy transition, we appear to be moving toward a more privatised system of infrastructure ownership', writes political economist Brett Christophers of Uppsala University in Sweden. In his book *Our Lives in Their Portfolio*, the professor analyses the rise of asset managers. 'Increasingly, the biggest investors in clean energy infrastructure are asset managers. For example, Canadian Brookfield Asset Management is one of the world's largest owners of renewable energy infrastructures'.[5] Christophers also talks about BlackRock. As we saw in the previous chapter, BlackRock was one of the winners of the 2008 banking crisis.

'Asset managers were some of the biggest lobbyists and interested parties behind the Inflation Reduction Act last year, which was about providing incentives for further private investment in US clean energy infrastructure. The ten-year extension of subsidies that have been put in place by the Inflation Reduction Act is one that asset managers actively lobbied for, and they have subsequently spoken about how enthused they are by those incentives.'[6]

The purported end of neoliberalism doesn't mean that the days of opening up markets, imposing privatisation and dismantling labour protections are behind us. The conditions being imposed on countries of the South to refinance their loans are as harshly neoliberal today as they ever were. The people of Pakistan and Argentina, among others, can attest to this.

Death to neoliberalism, the slogan tattooed on the Columbia University student's arm, is not taking us back to the days of big public investment. No, President Biden has not taken up Roosevelt's

5 Cal Turner and Sara Van Horn, An Interview with Brett Christophers - 'Asset Managers Like BlackRock Are Controlling More and More of Our Lives', *Jacobin*, 5 February 2023.
6 Ibid.

mantle, he is a dismantler of the New Deal legacy. Nor do his policies take us into a phase of fair-trade relations. Instead, they lock us further into bloc-building and protectionism. Washington's new industrial policy is not the 'end of neoliberalism' but the beginning of a new cold war. *Bidenomics*, as President Biden's economic policy has been dubbed, is really about prioritising geopolitical power interests over the prescriptions of market fundamentalism.

Rising hostility towards China is not an unfortunate by-product of a green transition, but the very essence of Bidenomics. According to the *New Left Review*, 'the logic governing the new era of infrastructure spending is fundamentally geopolitical; its precedent is to be sought not in the New Deal but in the military Keynesianism of the Cold War.'[7] We are on the cusp of a new phase, one that has not yet been aptly named. But it will be dominated by growing rivalry with a rising China.

7 Grey Anderson, 'Strategies of Denial', *New Left Review*, 15 June 2023.

From Energy Revolution to Trade War

*Chile has begun the definitive recovery of our most
fundamental source of wealth – copper. The nationalisation
of our copper is not an act of vengeance or hatred directed
towards any group, government, or nation. We are, on the
contrary, positively exercising an inalienable right on behalf of
a sovereign people – that of the full enjoyment of our national
resources exploited by our national labour and effort. The·
recovery of copper is a decision by the whole of Chile, and
we demand that all countries and governments respect the
unanimous decision of a free people.*

Salvador Allende, first speech to the Chilean parliament
after his election, 1970

Energy upheavals tend to shake up social relationships. Coal,
for example, provided the fire with which the Industrial Revolution
transformed Britain into a global empire. And oil has painted
the twentieth century in all its hues: from fuel and industrial
derivatives to war.

In 1901, when the British secured the lucrative contract that led
to the establishment of the Anglo-Persian Oil Company, they may
not have known that they were signing one of the biggest mineral
resource contracts in history. But they soon did. 'Controlling oil
supplies will be a primary war objective', wrote the secretary of the
British War Cabinet in World War I.[1] In 1916, while countless sons
of labourers and farmers were dying in the stinking trenches along
the Yser River, the Allied leadership was already drawing up a plan

1   Peter Frankopan, *De zijderoutes. Een nieuwe wereldgeschiedenis*, Amsterdam:
    Spectrum, 2023, p.397.

to divide the post-war world between the imperial powers with the secret Sykes-Picot Agreement. The war would last another two years. The treaty stipulated that, after the war, the French would be able to operate in Syria and Lebanon and the British in Mesopotamia, Palestine, and Suez. London knew exactly what was at stake: control of the oil fields in Persia and the Middle East, and the strategic Suez Canal.

For years after the war, depending on London's oil interests, the British installed or deposed rulers in Iraq, Persia, and Afghanistan. When President Mohammad Mossadeq took it upon himself to nationalise Iran's oil in 1953, Washington took up the imperial torch and organised a coup to overthrow Mossadeq's government. Coups have been supported, presidents deposed, wars waged. Suffice it to say that control over energy has played a rather crucial role in history.

Today, we are witnessing a new energy revolution. While it is true that fossil fuels will not disappear immediately, they should be phased out as soon as possible. The transition to a fossil-free world is irreversible. And there can be no energy transition without an upheaval in materials and infrastructure, putting pressure on global relations. A new race is on for precious resources like lithium, cobalt, and nickel. Major infrastructure projects are underway: wind farms, solar parks, hydrogen pools, and new transportation routes.

Meanwhile, a digital upheaval is shaking the planet and driving rapid development in machine learning, artificial intelligence, data and data protection, hardware accelerators, 5G and 6G communications networks, and the semiconductors needed to do it all.

The energy transition and the digital transformation represent a dual upheaval that quickly led to the start of a trade war.

On his first day as president of the United States, Donald Trump pulled no punches, saying, 'From this day forward, it's going to be only America first, American first'. It was January 2017.

In his blustering style, Trump advocated unabashed nationalism. His country had to become great again. High tariffs were imposed on foreign steel and aluminium with the aim of encouraging production in the United States. Trump unleashed a trade war on a scale not seen since World War II.

In a trade war, countries try to hit each other with economic sanctions and other measures: tariffs, import restrictions, currency adjustments, or domestic subsidies – not military but economic weapons. A levy is met with a countervailing levy, and the next import restriction is inevitably met with a counter-restriction on imports. Such clashes are at odds with the free trade agreements that have been the hallmark of capitalism for decades.

In 2017, the world watched aghast at so much protectionism coming out of Washington: did anyone have The Donald under control? Yet the import tariffs were no tomfoolery. They were part of a deliberate strategy to rival China. Less than three years later, US import tariffs had been imposed on some \$350 billion worth of Chinese imports. Beijing responded with \$100 billion worth of retaliatory measures against US exports.[2] Global free trade supporters thought Trump's sanctions and import tariffs would disappear once the erratic property tycoon had left the White House. Quite the opposite: his successor, Joe Biden, tightened the economic screws even further. Trade barriers to thwart rivals are erected under the banner of 'national security'.

In the technological race, the fastest no longer automatically leads. Whoever is the smartest at tripping up their opponents can win. World trade is thus becoming increasingly politicised. Harsh sanctions led by the United States are designed not only to protect US markets but, more importantly, to hinder China's technological and economic development. Calling China a 'systemic rival' implies that you have to eliminate your rival. That doesn't make

---

2   Pablo Fajgelbaum and Amit Khandelwal, 'The Economic Impacts of the US–China Trade War', *Annual Review of Economics*, Vol. 14: 205-228, August 2022.

the world a safer place. Let's look at the rivalry in three key areas: raw materials, artificial intelligence, and semiconductors.

RAW MATERIALS

In Mendeleev's periodic table, lithium is number three, cobalt is number twenty-seven, nickel is next to it at number twenty-eight, and graphite is made of carbon, which is number six. That's how I learnt it as a high school student in chemistry class. The truth is, I forgot it just as quickly. These four raw materials – lithium, cobalt, nickel, and graphite – are now economic staples. Indispensable for making batteries in an economy where batteries are crucial to the shift to low-carbon production. 'Today, the United States produces only 4 per cent of the lithium, 13 per cent of the cobalt, 0 per cent of the nickel, and 0 per cent of the graphite required to meet current demand for electric vehicles. Meanwhile, more than 80 per cent of critical minerals are processed by one country, China', said US national security advisor Jake Sullivan.[3]

Western leaders are watching China's rapid development of green technology with wide-eyed wonder. Industrial giants that have always relied on fossil fuels for their profits are suddenly facing competition from unexpected sources. Electrification is the Western world's big push for greener transport. It's a booming market: 15 per cent of the cars sold in the world today are already electric, and the market is now worth more than €400 billion. The production of sufficient batteries is crucial.

'Batteries are the Battlefield' is *Foreign Policy* magazine's first headline for 2023.[4] Washington's problem is this: China produces three-quarters of the world's batteries. The US wants to get its own

3 Jake Sullivan, 'Remarks by National Security Advisor Jake Sullivan on Renewing American Economic Leadership at the Brookings Institution', White House, 27 April 2023.
4 Christina Lu and Liam Scott, 'Batteries Are the Battlefield', *Foreign Policy*, 25 January 2023.

battery factories up and running as soon as possible, with generous government support from the Inflation Reduction Act. This is why most European battery development projects are under pressure.[5]

The European Union has been quick to respond. The European Battery Alliance, one of Europe's largest public-private partnerships, will now produce its own batteries.[6] Stellantis, Total and Mercedes, for example, will receive a combined €800 million from the French and German governments to develop a battery plant in northern France. It's not as if the three companies are short of cash. In 2022, they had combined profits of nearly €60 billion. However, subsidy wars are the perfect opportunity for big businesses to shamelessly play states off against each other.

Producing all these batteries obviously requires a lot more raw materials, such as nickel and lithium. Although mainly used to make steel, nickel is now being used to make batteries, too. Almost half of the world's nickel is mined in Indonesia. Exporting unprocessed raw nickel has been banned there since 2014. Indonesia wants to attract investment in smelting, battery manufacturing, and assembling electric vehicles, among other areas. This approach is bearing fruit. Much to the chagrin of the European automobile industry, Indonesia later announced an export ban on raw bauxite and copper concentrate. The European Union brought the case before the World Trade Organisation. 'This is not something we are doing out of the blue', says Investment Minister Bahlil Lahadalia. 'We are learning from our developed country counterparts, who in the past have resorted to these unorthodox policies.'[7] Europe must taste of its own medicine! Lahadalia gently points out that the United Kingdom banned exports of raw wool during the sixteenth century to stimulate its domestic textile industry. And that the

5 Transport & Environment, 'Two-thirds of European battery production at risk-analysis', 6 March 2023.
6 European Battery Alliance 250, eba250.com.
   https://www.eba250.com/over-eba250/netwerk/
7 Leslie Hook, Harry Dempsey and Ciara Nugent, 'The new commodity superpowers', *Financial Times*, 8 August 2023.

United States used high import taxes during the nineteenth and twentieth centuries to encourage more domestic manufacturing.

~ ~ ~

Lithium, or white gold, is another essential element for batteries. To meet growing demand, 40 times more lithium needs to be extracted in the next fifteen years.[8] The tension is mounting. Zimbabwe and Namibia have banned exports of their raw lithium and require at least one stage of local processing to add value. Chile has announced that when current contracts expire in 2030 and 2043, it will transfer control of two giant lithium mines in the Atacama Desert to the state. 'No more "mining for the few"' says young Chilean president Gabriel Boric, 'We have to find a way to share the benefits of our country among all Chileans'.[9] Two-thirds of the world's lithium reserves are in the Bolivia-Chile-Argentina lithium triangle. The United States has traditionally regarded the whole of Latin America as its backyard, with the right to do whatever it wants. It's no different today. The language is the same. A senior US Army official recently described the lithium triangle region as a matter of 'national security' for the United States.[10]

As soon as a country finds itself in the crosshairs of Washington's 'national security interests', all bets are off. It's also an issue in Bolivia. A week after the democratically elected government of Evo Morales announced that it intended to exploit Bolivia's lithium reserves for its own development, Morales was ousted. He was replaced by a government that did not stand in the way of Western lithium companies. US imperialism's big mouths don't even hide it. 'We will coup whoever we want! Deal with it!',

8 International Energy Agency, 'The Role of Critical Minerals in Clean Energy Transitions. World Energy Outlook Special Report', March 2022.

9 Leslie Hook, Harry Dempsey and Ciara Nugent, 'The new commodity superpowers', *Financial Times*, 8 August 2023.

10 Luigi Morris, 'SOUTHCOM Chief Aims to Increase Imperialist Plunder of Latin America's Resources', *Left Voice*, 26 January 2023.

tweeted Elon Musk, the CEO of the US firm Tesla, after the coup against Morales. Musk speaks his mind: he wants guaranteed access to cheap lithium for his Tesla batteries. When I first heard about it, I almost didn't believe it. That didn't happen, surely? But it did. On 24 July 2020, Elon Musk tweeted that a second US government stimulus package was 'not in the best interests of the people', to which someone replied: "You know what wasn't in the best interest of people? The US government organising a coup against Evo Morales in Bolivia so you could obtain the lithium there'. Musk then wrote: 'We will coup whoever we want! Deal with it'.[11] That, too, is the lithium war.

ARTIFICIAL INTELLIGENCE

On the fourth Thursday of March 2022, President Biden's Air Force One landed in Brussels. A US network broadcasted the landing live. Biden was in Brussels on a dual mission. He wanted to cash in on the energy deal, as we have seen, but just as importantly, he also wanted to break the European privacy shield. This digital shield was designed to protect European internet users' data from theft by large foreign corporations. The shield has been the topic of debate for three years. American big tech wants it gone. And preferably as soon as possible.[12]

Biden wanted to ensure that US companies do not lose access to data from the European market. This was the main purpose of his visit to Brussels. Indeed, the European Union objects to data from European users of Google, Amazon, and Facebook going straight to computer servers in the United States. That data then falls outside European jurisdiction.

Still, Biden got the job done. His big tech can now freely collect

---

11 teleSUR, 'Elon Musk Confesses to Lithium Coup in Bolivia', *Telesurenglish. net*, 25 July 2020.

12 Mark Scott and Vincent Manancourt, 'US eyes breakthrough on data dispute with EU as Biden visits Brussels', *Politico*, 24 March 2022.

and process the data of 400 million European consumers.

Data collection and digital technology are high on the political agenda. Washington has an edge in this area. Eight of the ten largest tech companies in the world are from the land of Uncle Sam.[13]

To stay ahead, tech giants can no longer rely on an army of whiz kids or clever programmers. It's all about data, data about anything you can imagine: where you've been, what you've bought, what you've almost bought, which websites you've browsed for a moment, which videos you've watched, which articles or videos you've liked, but also your heart rate, how often you exercise, how you drive your car, who you meet, and where you go on holiday. All this data is a predictor of your consumer behaviour. The new generation of computer programmes best at distilling predictions from the endless harvest of data is now called – because appearances can be deceiving – artificial intelligence, or AI for short. The best known is ChatGPT. With this programme, you can seemingly conjure up the most eloquent and powerful texts out of thin air. Based on your own prompts. This staggering technology runs on one resource: data. It's a huge database of online texts. By analysing all these texts, the AI system can guess the most likely answer to a given question, or, at least, the most likely text to follow the question, because such a system does not look at the content. Whether the answer is correct or not is another matter. You reap what you sow, and if the seed is mutated, the harvest will be too.

The race is on to develop the smartest AI programmes as quickly as possible. The only country capable of challenging US big tech is China. For every US giant, there's a Chinese counterpart. Instead of Google, you have Baidu as a search engine. After Amazon, Alibaba is the largest online shop. In China, you don't WhatsApp, you send messages through WeChat. Apple and Korea's Samsung are joined by Chinese smartphone makers Oppo, Xiaomi, Realme, Vivo, and, most recently, once again, Huawei.

13 Companiesmarketcap.com, 'Largest Companies by Market Cap', accessed on 19 June 2023.

Until recently, the technology market was still intertwined internationally. Free trade, of course. German machine manufacturers Siemens and Bosch have been working with Chinese technology companies for more than a decade to develop software and electronic circuits. The US firm Apple produces over 95 per cent of its devices in the People's Republic. And the booming Chinese market is a major source of profit for the US company.[14]

SEMICONDUCTORS

Without semiconductors – also known as chips – we would no longer be able to use apps, make phone calls, make payments, put milk in the fridge, toast bread, watch TV, or drive a car. A new car, for example, will soon have more than a thousand chips. As the brain of every electronic device and system, semiconductors are the lifeblood of the modern economy. They are also crucial building blocks for quantum computing and artificial intelligence innovations. ChatGPT is said to have been trained on tens of thousands of the most advanced chips on the market today.

Needless to say, no chips, no progress. And so, on 7 October 2022, Washington declared a chip war on Beijing. On that day, the United States announced its intention to completely cripple China's ability to produce, or even just purchase, semiconductors. You can't write it any clearer than *The New York Times*:

'Though delivered in the unassuming form of updated export rules, the Oct. 7 controls essentially seek to eradicate, root and branch, China's entire ecosystem of advanced technology.'[15]

Eradicate, root and branch, are punitive words. Allen Muse, a

14 Patrick McGee, 'How Apple Tied its Fortunes to China', *Financial Times*, 16 January 2023.
15 Alex W. Palmer, 'An Act of War: Inside America's Silicon Blockade Against China', *The New York Times Magazine*, 11 August 2023.

senior semiconductor analyst at Evercore ISI, tells the newspaper:

> 'If you'd told me about these rules five years ago, I would've told you that's an act of war – we'd have to be at war. . . .Not only are we not going to allow China to progress any further technologically, but we are going to actively reverse their current state of the art'.

The semiconductor specialist is in no doubt:

> 'There are two dates that will echo in history from 2022. The first is Feb. 24, when Russia invaded Ukraine; and the second is Oct. 7'.[16]

Producing semiconductors is one of the most complex manufacturing processes, not least because it involves dimensions so small that they are barely perceptible. It's no wonder that *fabs*, semiconductor fabrication plants, are the most expensive in the world. Only a handful of companies compete at the cutting edge here, with breakthroughs costing billions of dollars and decades of research. 'I truly believe our machine is the most complex thing that humans have ever made', Jos Benschop of the Dutch company ASML boasts. He may have a point. ASML builds the world's most advanced chip machines in Veldhoven, the Netherlands. The devices look like time machines. They are the technology of the future. Structures as small as 10 nanometres can be produced with the latest version of the extreme ultraviolet lithography machine. This is seven hundred times smaller than the diameter of a red blood cell. It's a scale that can hardly be grasped. The machine uses a laser to create plasma 40 times hotter than the sun's surface, emitting extreme ultraviolet light reflected by a series of mirrors on a silicon chip. What powerful technology!

16 Ibid.

Computer chips, or electronic circuits, are essential for building the most powerful computers. You need supercomputers like this to process large amounts of data. If you have the best supercomputer, you can do the best science. After all, supercomputers make it possible to run simulations on huge amounts of data. For example, to study the behaviour of colliding galaxies, to model the future of climate change, or to investigate the physics of hypersonic rockets. Semiconductors are at the root of it all.

By unilaterally banning exports on 7 October 2022, the United States was gambling. If other countries such as Taiwan, Japan, and the Netherlands continued to sell to China as usual, the US export ban would have been practically useless. With this in mind, the prime minister of the Netherlands, Marc Rutte, was summoned to the White House in early 2023. And that's where Rutte gives in. The United States gets its way; the Dutch ASML will no longer issue export licences to China.

It's no longer a question of protecting one's trade but of deliberately slowing down a rival. Emily Kilcrease, a former senior US trade official, makes no secret of it: 'We said there are key tech areas that China should not advance in', says Emily Kilcrease, 'and those happen to be the areas that will power future economic growth and development'.[17] But the story doesn't end there. 'If any country can overcome such a challenge, it is likely to be China', reports *The New York Times*:

'The Oct. 7 export controls, while crippling China's advanced chip-making ability for the foreseeable future, may end up spurring long-term growth'.[18]

In a major technological breakthrough, the Chinese company SMIC reportedly made the leap from 14 nm to 7 nm semiconductor chips.

17 Ibid.
18 Ibid.

~ ~ ~

Raw materials, artificial intelligence, data protection, semiconductors: where does the race end? Every sanction begets a countersanction, which changes the rules of the geopolitical game. The White House increasingly sees the battle with China as a zero-sum game in which you must choose sides, because an advantage for one side is bound to lead to an equal disadvantage for the other side(s). You are either with the United States against China or you are in the opposing camp. Washington is splitting the world into two blocs.

The more energy is devoted to thwarting the opponent, the more mutual development and cooperation suffer. Anyone who wants to reduce world trade to a zero-sum game, in which there is only one winner and one loser, is playing with fire. Bloc thinking, which reduces the world economy to two large rival blocs, does not benefit the planet.

If the Chinese economy were to completely decouple from the Western economies, it would cost the world 7 per cent of the wealth produced. To put this into context: that 7 per cent is approximately the impact of the corona crisis and the 2008 financial crisis combined. A decoupling from China would mean a 15 per cent loss for the European economy and a 20 per cent loss for the US economy. This is the International Monetary Fund's calculation.[19] Washington is aware of these figures, of course. This is why the White House keeps insisting that it's not a question of economic decoupling from China, but of 'derisking',[20] – a word coined by the president of the European Commission, Ursula von der Leyen.

---

19 Shekhar Aiyar et al, 'Geoeconomic Fragmentation and the Future of Multilateralism', Staff Discussion Notes No. 2023/001, International Monetary Fund, 15 January 2023.

20 Jami Miscik, Peter Orszag, and Theodore Bunzel, 'The U.S.-Chinese Economic Relationship Is Changing – But Not Vanishing. How 'De-Risking' Can Preserve Healthy Integration', *Foreign Affairs*, 24 May 2023.

But the goal of the US hawks remains the same: cutting off China from high-tech industries. 'De-risking is not really a great term', says Stefan Hartung. He is the head of Bosch, Europe's largest auto parts supplier. He isn't convinced about the growing hostility towards Beijing. 'You can't *de-risk* by isolating yourself', says the CEO.[21] The International Monetary Fund also warns against the increasing politicisation of world trade and the formation of blocs,

'The war has also increased the risk of a more permanent fragmentation of the world economy into geopolitical blocs with distinct technology standards, cross-border payment systems, and reserve currencies. Such a tectonic shift would entail high adjustment costs and long-run efficiency losses as supply chains and production networks are reconfigured.'[22]

But the politicisation continues. This is even evident in the use of language. 'The CHIPS Act invests $52 billion to restore U.S. leadership in semiconductor manufacturing. It is an investment larger than the real cost of the Manhattan Project', says US national security advisor Jake Sullivan to a science summit in 2022.[23] Sullivan refers, in passing, to the Manhattan Project. Why? To underline the Biden administration's level of investment? It certainly does that. But you can't help feeling that more and more cold war rhetoric is creeping into official discourse. The Manhattan Project was about the relationship between science and war, as anyone who has seen Christopher Nolan's film *Oppenheimer* will know. This ultra-secret project involved thousands of scientists working between 1942 and 1946 to develop the first atomic bomb, which was eventually

21 Patricia Nilsson, 'Bosch boss urges Europe to be more competitive and worry less about China', *Financial Times*, 29 July 2023.

22 IMF World Economic Outlook, War sets back the global recovery. IMF, April 2022, Washington DC, XIV

23 The White House, 'Remarks by National Security Advisor Jake Sullivan at the Special Competitive Studies Project Global Emerging Technologies Summit', Whitehouse.gov, 16 September 2022.

dropped on Hiroshima and Nagasaki. Jake Sullivan's subliminal message today is also: we're putting our scientists to work in a new cold war, not over nuclear fission, but over semiconductors and batteries.

But this cold war language gets us nowhere. Countries with large economies have a responsibility to respect other countries and treat them as equals. Large countries should be the first to base their relations with other countries on dialogue and partnership rather than confrontation or opportunistic alliance politics. We can overcome the challenges of this world by working together, not by building new walls. Fortunately, more and more forces are convinced of this.

The Abduction of Europe

The children of Agenor were playing
in a flower-filled meadow one afternoon,
when Europa wandered off and became separated from her
brothers.
Her eye had been caught by a beautiful white bull
grazing in the long grass.
The bull's breath was sweet and its nose soft and strokeable.
Then, without quite knowing why,
she lifted herself onto its back.
They didn't stop until they reached the island of Crete
where the bull made itself known as....
...who else but Zeus?

Stephen Fry, *Mythos* ('The Abduction of Europa')

Chancellor Olaf Scholz announced a U-turn in German foreign policy three days after the war broke out in Ukraine. A reset was imminent, he said, because we were at a turning point or tipping point, a *Zeitenwende* in German. It was the German buzzword of the year in 2022. In Belgium, 'energy poverty' was the expression that emerged as the winner. It's a turning point, says Scholz. But to where?

In the last three great continental wars, Germany and France were militarily at each other's throats. After the Second World War, there was a growing belief that peace between the two European powers was crucial to the future of the continent. This conviction gave birth to European unification. From then on, Paris and Berlin would exchange words, not bullets. And that's what they have been doing ever since: seeking compromise. One of the basic conditions was no more German pin helmets, *Stahlhelme* or Panzers. Future military protection was for France, the only nuclear power on the continent with a serious military and with a seat on the UN Security Council. The trade-off was the economy for Germany.

The euro, the European currency, was cast in the nickel of the Deutsche Mark, and the Germans controlled monetary policy from Frankfurt. At the expense of other countries on the continent, they worked their way up to become world export champions. When the euro crisis hit in 2011, nothing happened without Berlin's blessing.

One the military, the other the economy. Somewhat of an oversimplification, but this division of labour was at the heart of the new European idea. Of course, there were rumblings between Berlin and Paris at every step of European unification. The Germans preached stability and austerity; the French saw more merit in government intervention and growth.

The war in Ukraine unsettled all relations. A *Zeitenwende*. Russian gas was the mainstay of German industry and exports for years. However, war and sanctions put an end to that, destroying a crucial ingredient for German dominance. Berlin is left scrambling for alternatives. France, by contrast, runs 70 per cent on nuclear power, which currently benefits Paris. France's military complex is, moreover, much more advanced than Germany's. In response, some forces in Berlin are increasingly playing the US card.

However, in economic terms, Germany is still the only real giant. In 2008, the country's GDP was around €500 billion higher than France's. Today, that gap has widened to over a trillion euros. Manufacturing accounts for just under 11 per cent of France's gross domestic product, compared with 27 per cent in Germany. Germany remains Europe's industrial heavyweight.

~~~

There are two bones of contention between Berlin and Paris. The first dispute is about energy. Paris wants an energy price cap for the whole of the European Union; Berlin wants nothing of the sort. Berlin would have liked a gas pipeline between Spain and Germany, the MidCat, but Macron single-handedly blocked it. He found it far too expensive. Germany decided to allocate €200 billion to reduce energy prices for businesses and households unilaterally. Chancellor Scholz announced that decision out of the blue at the European Council without consulting other member states. Germany's bombshell led to misunderstanding.

The second bone of contention involves defence. Since 2017, France's Dassault and Germany's Airbus have been working on an air defence project called the Future Combat Air System, or FCAS. However, the project is in danger of being derailed because Dassault is reluctant to share its technological know-how. The plan to jointly build new tanks to replace the Leopard 2 and Leclerc battle tanks also seems to have run aground. German metals giant Rheinmetall has come up with an alternative of its own. Berlin is not waiting for the FCAS to arm itself and is procuring 35 US F-35 jets. The United States makes a shrewd move, promising to have Rheinmetall build certain parts for all F-35s. Paris reacts furiously as French arms manufacturers are left out in the cold. Washington, meanwhile, is the laughing third party.

'European sovereignty will be possible only if France and Germany come together. This will require further additional efforts', writes French foreign expert Landry Charrier and German security expert Hans-Dieter Heumann in a joint opinion piece. 'In the end, however, there will be no other option: strategic autonomy is and remains "a process of political survival" for safeguarding Europe's vital interests'.[1] Of course, the United States is skilfully trying to stir up tensions on the old continent, and the Franco-

1 Landry Charrier and Hans-Dieter Heumann, 'Franco-German Perspectives: Europe's Moment of Geopolitics', Globalgovernance.eu, June 2023.

German engine is sputtering. However, both countries need each other to secure Europe's future. If the Paris-Berlin axis allows itself to be torn apart by Washington, the European project will perish. In Europe, we face tensions that will open a Pandora's box from which only nationalist monsters can emerge.

What Now, Europe?

French president Emmanuel Macron's visit to China at the end of April 2023 caused a stir. The news headlines were scathing for Macron. 'Macron's visit to China is a complete disaster', is the headline on Dutch radio BNR news. 'Macron's China trip turns into a European uproar', headlines *The Washington Post*. Domestically, the French president has been under fire for a year for pushing through a new pension law almost by force of arms, briefly suspending parliament and ordering the army and police to crush the unions' persistent protests. Did his state visit to China serve as a lightning rod? Perhaps. But this interpretation of the facts is far too superficial. Much more was at play below the waterline.

A much longer debate has been going on about how Europe should act in a changing world. Entire bookshelves have been written about it. No surprise, then, that the French president said in Beijing that Europe wants nothing to do with the growing hostility between the United States and China. Arguing for an autonomous Europe as a third power, Macron said, 'I don't believe in a world of two hostile blocs, East and West'. The harsh reactions to his remarks are indicative of the current climate. The climate is increasingly one of 'campism'. Those who do not take sides are immediately banished.

Anyone able to impose their language on the debate already has a major strategic advantage. These words of wisdom are from the Italian communist Antonio Gramsci, who was thrown into prison by Mussolini's fascist regime. Language matters, words matter.

Some hawks in Washington, for example, like to talk about

a 'new cold war'. This isn't innocent talk; in a cold war, you have to choose sides. No one benefits from such a binary view of the world: zero or one, on or off, one or the other.

More and more oil is being poured on the fire. 'Tensions with China may have been more visible under Trump, but they are even more intense under Joe Biden', remarks a Belgian tech entrepreneur. He fears that the pressure on European companies to take sides will only increase, 'The United States is strongly polarising the chip issue. And Europe is under pressure to go along with that narrative'.[1] Martin Quencez, a researcher at the German Marshall Fund in Paris, shares this view. 'Europe has become an object in global competition rather than an issue', Quencez warns. 'We must avoid getting into a Cold War 2.0 where countries must choose between two options. That's counterproductive. We have to make it clear that we are willing to be pragmatic and compromise, that we don't close the door immediately if we dislike something'.[2]

~~~

Europe's relationship with China differs from Uncle Sam's. Washington is largely self-sufficient in energy, remains technologically superior, and has enormous military power. From that hegemonic position, it can allow itself more protectionism. Europe is in a different position. As German industry knows, the country's prosperity is based on its export strength, and that requires free world trade. Europe and China have become economically intertwined in recent decades, becoming each other's most important partners. This bilateral trade is worth almost €700 billion.

China is also a top supplier of semiconductors, rare-earth

---

1 'Conflict tussen VS en China plaatst Europese bedrijven voor moeilijke keuzes', *De Tijd*, 25 April 2023.
2 Erik Ziarczyk, 'Oorlog in Oekraïne legt fundamenten multipolaire wereldorde bloot', *De Tijd*, 23 May 2023.

elements, and raw materials such as lithium and cobalt – crucial for building batteries for wind turbines, solar panels, and electric cars. Without help from China, Europe will never achieve climate neutrality by 2050. The Dutch Clingendael Institute has studied the links between the European and Chinese economies. 'Complete decoupling from China is not realistic. This would come at a high economic cost for the European Union', says researcher Frans-Paul van der Putten. For him, the way forward is clear, 'Europe needs to stand up and be counted when it comes to the US and China. It is important that we are not forced to adopt the US-China policy.'[3]

The big boss of German chemical giant BASF thinks so too:

'Europe is really hit the most. That has to do with the Ukraine war. We need to make cuts. Activities requiring a lot of energy will be discontinued. BASF still has 40 per cent of its business in Europe and needs to participate in the Asian market. China is the key, as it will be in control of half of the global market by 2030. Three-quarters of all growth will then come from China. The biggest risk is the growing geopolitical conflict between China and the US. We're hoping for a pragmatic solution, as driving China into a corner is not the solution.'[4]

Author Pascal Coppens makes a similar point. He is an expert on China and has spent a lot of time there. He told the financial newspaper *De Tijd*:

'China wants to reduce the pressure and restore relations, but the trend in Washington is very different. China is not isolating

3 Lieve Dierckx and Piet Depuydt, 'China ontlopen in de wereldhandel is onmogelijk', *De Tijd*, 29 October 2022.
4 Martin Brudermüller, chairman of the Board of Executive Directors, BASF. In this WPC Executive Conversation, Martin Brudermüller, chairman and CEO of BASF, discusses petrochemicals market demand. https://players.brightcove.net/6178286504001/default_default/index.html?videoId=6323156834112

itself. The United States is forcing China into isolation. That's an important distinction'.[5]

~~~

A non-aligned Europe is better off. However, there is a snag with Macron's call for the European Union to become a third power. Trio-bloc thinking is no answer to the duo-bloc thinking of Washington versus Beijing. Macron's statement represents the voice of one of the EU's most important industrial interest groups. A group that has long wanted to build a highly competitive Europe. That desire has always existed. 'Europeans and European industry want European leaders to ensure that their voices are heard in the global concert', the powerful lobby group European Round Table said on the eve of the euro's launch.[6] And who can forget that in March 2000, European leaders drew up a plan to make Europe 'the most competitive knowledge-based economy in the world'? This meant overhauling the labour market, liberalising the public sector, and reducing wage costs. The result is well-known. Instead of the most competitive economy in the world, we had years of austerity that led to the euro crisis of 2011.

Some of the same old voices are dreaming again of their own European imperialist project, with its own protectionism and its own rat race for precious resources in the Global South, enabling it to take part in a new cold war from a position of strength. This European imperialist project serves nobody, neither the Global South nor the working class of the old continent itself.

If we want to be non-aligned in Europe, we have to be democratic so that it is not done to allocate massive amounts of public money to large private monopolies but to build the European sectors of the future as public sectors. That's the 'doe-de-switch'

5 Lieve Dierckx and Piet Depuydt. 'China ontlopen in de wereldhandel is onmogelijk'. *De Tijd*, 29 October 2022.
6 Cited in Peter Mertens. Hoe durven ze, o.c. p.169.

(make the switch) programme we advocate. A non-aligned Europe cannot exist without diversifying its political and commercial relations. The more partners Europe loses, the more we depend on one other country. Rather than locking ourselves into blocs or 'strategic alliances', engaging in a wide range of relationships is better. Only then will we be better equipped to resist extortion and not give in to those who want to cut the EU off from other parts of the world. A non-aligned Europe needs fair trade and cooperation. Many critical raw materials come mainly from the countries of the South. We don't need lithium, cobalt, uranium, or hydrogen colonialism at the bidding of major private players from Europe. If Europe wants to build a future, it must base its relations on fair trade agreements. We are stronger when we work together.

Europe stubbornly refused to share vaccine technology with countries of the South during the pandemic. Sharing green technology and insulation techniques can help countries of the South accelerate their ecological transition. This will benefit everyone, including those in the North. Europe should not allow itself to be abducted by white bulls from across the ocean. It is better off forging its own path.

Chapter 4

Mutiny

Brasilia

La esperanza es como las fichas del dominó:
cuando una cae,
acaban cayendo todas
Hope is kind of like dominoes.
Once one falls,
the rest follow.
    Tokyo in Money Heist (*La casa de papel*)

In January 1955, Belgium hosted wind tunnel tests. Not for cyclists, cars, or planes, but for spheres. Large steel spheres with aluminium cladding. This involved calculating how the spheres would resist the wind. And it had to happen quickly. The spheres were part of the Belgian showpiece, the Atomium, at the 1958 Brussels World's Fair. As this left little time for design and build, the Atomium was designed as a Meccano kit. All these standardised parts meant that the project could go ahead. The builders, architects, and planners succeeded. The Atomium was completed on 25 March 1958, a mere three weeks before Expo 58 opened, from drawing board to opening in just four years. We're extremely proud of that as Belgians. Our Atomium – which lends colour to Brussels along with the bronze fountain statue of Manneken Pis – is still looking good after its renovation.

At the time of the Atomium, another feat of engineering was taking place 8,900 kilometres from Brussels. It's fair to say that this construction project was even more challenging: the creation of an entirely new capital city within four years. The story goes that, in 1956, Brazilian president Juscelino Kubitschek told Oscar Niemeyer, the famous architect from Rio de Janeiro, during a car ride, 'I will build a new capital for this country: more central, in the interior, to strengthen the unity of the country. And I need you to help me'. The master builder immediately launched a competition. Niemeyer, who was a communist, wanted to collect as many ideas as he could.

After a year of searching for a partner, Niemeyer finally settled on his old friend, the architect Lúcio Costa. Niemeyer and Costa were given a tight deadline: the new capital was to be inaugurated on 21 April 1960, a national holiday. Architects and builders had three years to design and build the city. In just three years, the government and administrators would meet there, guests would sleep in its hotel rooms, and people would make it their home. As no site had been chosen for the new capital, Niemeyer and his team boarded a plane to look for the right place from the air. He noticed a central plateau with a natural wetland. It was there, in the sparsely populated centre of the country, that the futuristic city – Brasilia – would soon emerge.

I spent a short time in Brasilia at the end of 2005. It was an eye-opener for me. Everywhere I went, I soaked up the architectural spirit of Le Corbusier. I'd been invited to attend the Congress of the Brazilian Communist Party (*Partido Comunista Brasileiro*, PCdoB), the Communist Party that took part in President Luiz Inácio 'Lula' da Silva's first government. How do you achieve your own Brazilian development in a rapidly changing world? That was the discussion, even then. And it was a lively affair, with participants from all corners of the vast country. I recall how the Amazon delegation had been on the road to Brasilia longer than it had taken me to travel from Brussels. On the second day, President Lula arrived, and I found the former union leader quite formidable.

During his two terms in office, the former union leader and now President focused on developing production and improving health and education. Minimum wages rose, and more than a million jobs were created. The Food and Agriculture Organisation calculated that malnutrition fell by 73 per cent under Lula.

When the former metalworker retired in 2011, he still had an 80 per cent approval rating. But Brazil's right-wing forces from big landowner circles got even with him in 2018. The former president was jailed on corruption charges. Brazil's Supreme Court would later overturn all of Lula's convictions. When Lula was deprived of his freedom, the landless rural workers' movement, the MST, responded immediately. They set up camp right outside the prison, shouting 'Good morning, Lula!' towards his cell every morning. The MST strongly opposed the far-right president Jair Bolsonaro, who gained power in 2018 with the help of Big Agro. His drastic health policies during the pandemic, the destruction of the rainforest, and the attack on the rights of Indigenous peoples met with widespread opposition from social movements. Lula also fought back. He regained the presidency with a slim majority at the end of 2022. Lula can chart Brazil's course to independence. But he will have to remain on his guard against Bolsonaro's loudest supporters.

~~~

Brazil covers about half of South America and has a population of 208 million, making it the seventh most populous country in the world. It's no lightweight. Yet it is not part of the leading group of industrialised countries, called the G7, because there are, well, seven of them: the United States, Canada, the United Kingdom, France, Germany, Italy, and Japan, plus the European Union. The G7 emerged in the wake of the 1970s oil crisis, establishing itself as the world's economic and political headquarters for the past four decades. Apart from industrialised Japan, only Western countries had a seat at G7 meetings.

That changed in early 2023. Lula was invited to the G7 summit in Hiroshima, Japan. Lula was not the only emerging economy guest. Government leaders from Indonesia, Vietnam, Australia, South Korea, and India were also invited. Lula did not go to

Hiroshima to toe the line or follow the script. It's not in his trade union blood to play such a passive role. At the press conference, he stunned friends and foes alike by talking about. . . football. Lula mentioned Vinicius Junior's fortunes at Real Madrid, condemning the racism faced by Brazilian and other footballers in Europe. The press room fell silent. He took advantage of that to keep going. Brazil must become a full-fledged player on the world economic stage, said the president with understated pride. Our country should not be leashed – to anyone. 'I don't want a cold war between China and the United States, where we fall victim to their rivalry. I want free trade where everyone can negotiate, buy, and sell with anyone they want'. The Brazilian president's confidence signals the cusp of a new era, an era in which the countries of the South are making their voices heard.

~~~

In 2008, the collapse of the US investment bank Lehman Brothers triggered a global financial crisis. It highlighted the vulnerability of the West's financial institutions. Surely, it's not wise to rely so much on fragile institutions, reasoned those in the South. Before you know it, you're also ensnared. Taking the bull by the horns, several major developing countries joined forces the following year. The five-nation group became known as 'the BRICS' after the first letters of their names – Brazil, Russia, India, China, and South Africa, five major emerging countries on four continents. Together with Indonesia, Mexico, Nigeria, and others, in 2009, they began to think about reviving the South–South cooperation agenda. To recap, the renewed South–South agenda was born in response to the banking crisis in the North.

It was only a matter of time until it finally happened, in May 2023. It was a tipping point largely hidden from Northern eyes. The Global South's share of global GDP exceeded that of the North for the first time in centuries. As for the share of the global economy, the G7 has been overtaken this year by a group of emerging economies, of which Brazil is a member: the BRICS.[1]

The freedom to make your own way through the geopolitical minefield is contagious. At the end of August 2023, the BRICS welcomed six new members: Argentina, Egypt, Ethiopia, Iran, Saudi Arabia, and the United Arab Emirates (Argentina opted out after an election that brought to power a man from the far-right). This brings the BRICS partnership to almost half of the world's population and over a third of the global GDP. Indonesia, a global giant in terms of gross domestic product, withdrew its candidacy at the last minute, but is still considering joining. Forty other countries have also expressed interest in signing up, including seven of the thirteen members of OPEC, the Organisation of the Petroleum Exporting Countries.

The desire to formulate their own policies based on their national interests is what unites the BRICS countries in all their diversity. It's not a moral question, but a very pragmatic one. The countries of the Global South are asserting their place at the world table, albeit in a world where the major international institutions by no means mirror global relations. Permanent seats on the United Nations Security Council are still reserved for the victors of the Second World War. Neither Africa nor Latin America have a permanent member. Nor does India, the world's most populous country. Countries of the South don't exactly have their say at the International Monetary Fund either.

Whether you're in favour of BRICS-plus or not, the fact is that world relations are in a state of flux, moving towards a new form of non-alignment in the Global South, which expresses itself politically in a variety of shades.

---

1 *The Economist*, 'Can the West win over the rest of the world?', 16 May 2023.

The Spirit of Bandung

Without economic liberation, the freedom of non-aligned
countries will be neither real nor complete.
> Indira Gandhi, Prime Minister of India, 1973

Koen Bogaert is a modest and naturally cheerful man: neither loud nor pushy, but intense. I met him when he was young, back in 2010, when we formed a Socialist Round Table with the late professor Jan Blommaert, the theatre producer Dominique Willaert, and several other 'heathens'. We organised the Days for Socialism together at the Vooruit in Ghent and at De Singel in Antwerp. Koen Bogaert knows what he's talking about. He works in the Department of Conflict and Development Studies at Ghent University, where he lectures on colonial history and decolonial resistance. I see him again in the summer of 2023 to talk about his first book: *In het spoor van Fanon (On the Trail of Fanon)*.[1] His book transports you to the slave plantations, the powerful Haitian revolution, and the anti-colonial resistance of working-class women in nineteenth-century Manchester. 'All anyone talks about here in Europe is the French Revolution', Koen tells me in the cultural basement of the De Groene Waterman bookshop. 'But who talks about the Haitian revolution? Its size and importance can't be overestimated'.

It's hardly taught in schools, but two years after the French Revolution, the Haitian people rebelled against their French colonial masters. This was the first successful anti-colonial uprising in which Black revolutionaries defeated the French, British, and

1 Koen Bogaert, *In het spoor van Fanon. Orde, wanorde, dekolonisering*, EPO, Berchem, 2023.

Spanish – and then the French again – before declaring Haiti's independence. Just as the French Revolution represents the advancement of the bourgeoisie in Europe, the Haitian Revolution represents the advancement of anti-colonialism and human rights struggles for all people. 'You know, Peter, Napoleon Bonaparte lost more men at Saint-Domingue than he did a decade later at Waterloo', Koen explains. He recounts the shock and anger of the elites in Washington and Paris, because uprisings also broke out on plantations in other colonies. Haiti was a living inspiration everywhere. For years, people in European metropoles were led to believe that the existing world was the only world possible and that the historical destiny of European powers was to colonise and bring other countries to heel. Britain controlled India and Egypt, the French held West Africa and Vietnam, the Dutch ruled Indonesia, the Portuguese governed Brazil, and the Belgians brutalised the Congo. Whether the territories were privately held by the Crown, governed by European armies, or owned by private companies such as the Dutch East India Company, the recipe was the same: raw materials were looted from the land. Until the Haitian revolution sent another message. More than resistance, because that had always been there, it was a message of victory.

The Haitian victory was the wind in the sails of freedom movements around the world. In the long nineteenth century, anti-colonial protests came of age. In 1927, several leaders met in Brussels for the first League Against Imperialism. Their aim was to create a platform that would unite the visions of anti-colonial movements in Africa, Asia, and Latin America. The Second World War put an end to that. But ultimately, the war would be a game-changer. Imperial countries like Britain, France, the Netherlands, and Belgium emerged exhausted and weakened from the conflict. Hadn't the peoples of the whole world done their bit to fight fascism? No more fascism, no more war! But no exploitation and no colonial oppression, either! The colonies demanded their independence. Despite the brutal, bloody repression by Dutch troops in Indonesia, the French army in Algeria and British troops in India, there was no turning back. Dozens of countries gained independence in the 1950s and 1960s.

But the initial enthusiasm was soon to wane. In a world dominated by skewed relationships, it quickly became clear that being sovereign was not enough. World relations were still skewed, and that needed to change. In 1955, several countries of the South came together and pooled their ideas in the city of Bandung on the Indonesian island of Java. Anti-colonial leaders such as Jawaharlal Nehru of India, Achmed Sukarno of Indonesia, Zhou Enlai of China, and Gamal Abdel Nasser of Egypt rallied behind a platform that would later evolve into the Non-Aligned Movement. *Non-aligned* can be defined as being 'not politically aligned' or 'without a permanent partner'. The sovereign countries of the South refused to be locked in a bipolar political world assigned to either a capitalist bloc or a socialist bloc. Not wanting to be tied to one partner, they looked for an alternative. Alongside the 'First World' (capitalism), and the 'Second World' (socialism), they proudly presented themselves as the 'Third World' with a voice that wanted to be heard.

Peace, Bread, and Justice

'The "Third World" was not a place, Peter. It was a project: a project for more planetary democracy', Vijay Prashad tells me. We're having coffee in the canteen of the *Volksbühne* people's theatre on Rosa-Luxemburg-Platz in Berlin. I've come to meet him in the German capital to talk about this book. 'It will all work out with your book', he laughs. I wasn't feeling so convinced that day.

Vijay is a gifted speaker. I first met him through LeftWord Books. He published the English edition of my last book. The Indian historian and journalist has penned several classics on the Global South. His book *The Darker Nations* bowled me over.[1] It chronicles the tumultuous history of the rise of the 'non-aligned' countries, for this is not the first time that the countries of the South have had their backs to the wall. Vijay explains,

'The Bandung dynamic in 1955 ushered in the "Third World Project", a platform of the non-aligned countries.

'It sought to provide a future for humanity, all humanity, including the young nations and peoples of the South. Countries no longer wanted to be the serfs of their colonial masters. They wanted to be heard and empowered on the world stage'.

During this time, the North was only pointing an admonishing finger at 'internal factors' in the countries of the South. No mention was being made of structural world relations. And then came the platform of the non-aligned nations, proud and unashamed, built

1 Vijay Prashad, *The Darker Nations*, The New Press, New York, 2007.

around three major themes – peace, bread, and justice.

The first corner of the triangle was peace. The nuclear mushroom cloud over Hiroshima was still fresh in people's minds, the Korean War had just ended, and the arms race between the two superpowers was rapidly taking on dramatic proportions. The threat of the Cold War made everyone long for peace.

The second corner was bread. The newly independent nations each inherited an impoverished country with no social structures. Famine struck, and the fledgling economies of the South were forced to export. With little access to finance, technology and science, industrialisation and diversification, their economic arms were twisted to ensure that they would remain mono-economies focused on exporting. Failing to change these external factors also made internal change extremely difficult. Raúl Prebisch, an Argentinian economist, called for a 'new order in the international economy . . . so that the market functions properly not only for the big countries but also for the developing countries in their relations with the developed'.[2] Prebisch was pressing for a revision of the international free trade agenda, better commodity prices, and the transfer of investment and technology to the South.

The third corner was justice. Although the young nations were independent, proud, and sovereign, their voices were disregarded in the world's institutions. The five permanent Security Council members had hijacked the United Nations. The International Monetary Fund and the World Bank were in the hands of the Atlantic powers, and the General Agreement on Tariffs and Trade – GATT – was designed to thwart any attempt at a fair economic order. 'Are we only going to continue to be veranda boys?', the Nigerian foreign minister quite rightly asked. The non-aligned countries wanted more than a place in the kitchen or on the veranda. They wanted a seat at the decision-making table.

2 Vijay Prashad, *The Poorer Nations: A Possible History of the Global South*, Verso, London, 2014, pp.3-4.

~~~

Peace, bread, and justice. The industrialised nations saw things differently. They pulled out all the stops to keep emerging countries from progressing. All the stops. The countries of the South turned to the UN General Assembly as their last resort. And they were heard. Half a century ago, on 1 May 1974, the United Nations adopted an ambitious declaration on a much-needed 'New International Economic Order', or NIEO. Its key principles were non-interference in the internal affairs of others, full sovereignty over natural resources, a fair relationship between the price of commodities for exports and imports, and access to finance and technology. These are all just and fair principles. However, the West made their response to the UN's new agenda known. The NIEO had to be stopped, said German chancellor Helmut Schmidt, because leaving decisions about the global economy 'to officials somewhere in Africa or some Asian capital is not a good idea'. British Prime Minister Harold Wilson suggested that instead of giving African and Asian leaders a say, serious decisions would be best left to 'the sort of people sitting around this table'.[3]

That table was at the Château de Rambouillet, near Paris, and the people around it were men in ties and tie-clips from wealthy countries of the North, plus someone from Japan – the representatives of the G7. They had rallied together in Rambouillet in November 1975 to prevent a merger between the rich oil-producing OPEC countries and the sovereign aspirations of the non-aligned countries.

The Non-Aligned Movement was considered a 'mutiny' against the world order. And the G7 wanted nothing to do with the United Nations' declaration of a 'new international economic order'. Chancellor Helmut Schmidt spoke plainly: 'It is desirable to explicitly state that the present world recession is not a particularly

3 Ibid, p.42.

favourable occasion to work out a new economic order along the lines of certain UN documents.[4] United Nations declarations are all well and good unless they go against our interests.

4 Ibid, p.42.

La Década Perdida

The debt crisis of the 1980s derailed the momentum of the Non-Aligned Movement. It all began with Mexico's default in 1982. To understand this, we need to step back in time.

When the colonies forced their way to independence, the new nations inherited economies that were in the doldrums and countries with no state structures or social services to speak of. They needed money. The former colonial powers turned up with development aid to redeem themselves. But it was not enough. The young nations had to take out additional loans from governments and banks in the rich countries. And so, debt became the new means of controlling former colonies. The North increasingly viewed lending money to the South as a cash cow, funding many useful but many more useless projects. Loans to Latin American and African countries quadrupled. Faced with a rapidly rising debt burden, they were effectively forced to focus on commodity exports. It was the only way to bring in hard currency and pay off their debts.

Then, in 1981, Paul A. Volcker, the chair of the US Federal Reserve, raised the federal interest rate to 20 per cent. The shock sent the United States into a recession. However, the effects were also felt in the South. Owing to 'the highest real interest rates since the birth of Christ', as the ever-eloquent Chancellor Helmut Schmidt put it, the debtor countries were drowning in stratospheric borrowing costs. To make matters worse, commodity prices collapsed in the early 1980s. Even more had to be done for the dollars so urgently needed to meet the interest payments. For many countries, the blow was too much. Mexico was the first country to raise the alarm in 1982. It could not possibly continue

147

to repay its debts, and national bankruptcy was inevitable. Other countries would follow suit.

This was when two international institutions took a leading role: the International Monetary Fund and the World Bank. Both institutions had been created in the aftermath of the Second World War, to organise world trade, and the reins were firmly held by Washington. In the 1980s, the International Monetary Fund came under the influence of University of Chicago hardliners: Milton Friedman's school of economics. The IMF became the global credit community's enforcer. It was the only institution still lending to countries in arrears. These loans were subject to onerous conditions, with 'structural adjustment programmes' imposing cuts in spending on education and health, as well as in public food and fuel subsidies in these countries. Government institutions were also privatised. In short, the whole economy was reorganised in line with the rules set by Washington. British economist John Toye later labelled this approach a 'counter-revolution', a revolution against the spirit of the Non-Aligned Movement.[1] No more demands for structural justice. From then on, it was all about individual responsibility: internal reforms, internal liberalisation of trade and labour market regulations.

~~~

Today, people in Europe also understand what this means. Greece was subjected to harsh measures in 2011 in exchange for debt restructuring. The Greek government was forced to slash wages and pensions and sell off public companies for a pittance. The IMF also demanded that Greece limit its health spending to 6 per cent of GDP, while other European countries typically spend 10 per cent. Unmet healthcare needs in Greece reached

---

1 John Toye, *Dilemmas of Development: Reflections on the Counter-Revolution in Development Theory and Policy*, Oxford, Blackwell, 1987. Cited in: Tricontinental, file no. 66, July 2023, p.24

dramatic proportions.[2] Austerity cuts wiped out a quarter of the Greek economy, and Europe plunged into recession. But this is a story with far greater resonance in the South. To qualify for loans, dozens of countries were forced to jeopardise their public health, education, and public wealth and to open up their local economies to large corporations from the North. Sovereignty was often reduced to little more than a piece of paper.

The debt tragedy turned the 1980s into *la década perdida*, the lost decade for the South. UNICEF's calculations show that at least $20 billion flowed from South to North in 1989, compared with a net transfer of $40 billion from North to South a decade earlier. Any attempt to break with the orthodoxy of the International Monetary Fund was met with a relentless series of sanctions, including a nod to international creditors to stop lending. But not everyone was so willing to allow this to happen. Where injustice reigns, resistance awakens. IMF riots erupted across the South in the 1980s.

On 28 July 1987, a slender man wearing an olive-green uniform addressed the Organisation of African Unity meeting held in Addis Ababa, Ethiopia:

'Under its current form, controlled and dominated by imperialism, debt is a skilfully managed reconquest of Africa intended to subjugate its growth and development through foreign rules. Thus, each one of us becomes the financial slave, which is to say, a true slave of those who had been treacherous enough to put money in our countries with obligations for us to repay.'

Everyone in the room in Addis Ababa knew that the man dressed in olive green was right, but few dared to say it out loud. The man went by the name of Thomas Sankara and he was president

2 See David Stuckler and Sanjay Basu, *The Body Economic: Why Austerity Kills*, Allen Lane. 2013.

of Burkina Faso. When Sankara said that his country would refuse to pay its foreign debts, everyone held their breath. You could hear a pin drop. 'If Burkina Faso stands alone in refusing to pay, I will not be here for the next conference!', Sankara announced. Three months later, Sankara was dead – he'd been murdered. But the legacy of 'Africa's Che Guevara' and his quest for freedom lives on.

~~~

Alongside the debt crisis, another factor that derailed the non-alignment drive was the collapse of the Soviet Union in 1991. Having defeated fascism on 8 May 1945, the Soviet Union had emerged from the war as a new giant, much to the envy of Washington. Two years after the liberation from fascism, the Cold War was already a reality. The world was divided into two blocs: the US sphere and the Soviet sphere of influence. This bipolar moment in history ended in 1991 with the collapse of the Soviet Union. And with it, seemingly, the premise of the non-aligned movement. Meanwhile, confetti was flying in the United States. Some lofty intellectuals proclaimed it to be the end of history; they meant the beginning of a unipolar world, led by a single pole: the United States. From then on, Washington would be the world's policeman.

At our wooden table in Berlin's Volksbühne canteen, Vijay Prashad weighs his words,

'You know, Peter, leadership brings responsibility. It's not just about shouting and cursing. We were told that the most important power in the world would provide development and security.

'But the facts show that the opposite occurred. Inequality in the world has grown, as shown by all the human development indicators. You don't need Thomas Piketty for that.'

Amid growing inequality, insecurity – not security – became the name of the game. Vijay lays it all out for me: the war in Iraq, the global war on terror, and the war on drugs destabilising countries in Central America and the Andean region. He concludes,

'The question is not whether the United States should have been a world leader. But if you set out to lead, you have to live up to what's expected of you. Those expectations were not met. Instead of development, there was inequality. Instead of security, there was permanent instability.'

The brief unipolar moment in history is now behind us. The question is – what will replace it.

Watershed Moments

D'autres avant moi ont dit, d'autres après moi diront à quel point s'est élargi le fossé entre les peuples nantis et ceux qui n'aspirent qu'à manger à leur faim, boire à leur soif, survivre et conserver leur dignité. Mais nul n'imaginera à quel point le grain du pauvre a nourri chez nous la vache du riche.
Others before me have said, and others after me will say, how wide the gap has become between the affluent and those who aspire only to eat their fill, quench their thirst, survive and retain their dignity. But no one can imagine the extent to which the poor man's grain has fed the rich man's cow.
Thomas Sankara

'Europe is a garden. Everything works. It is the best combination of political freedom, economic prosperity, and social cohesion that humankind has been able to build. Most of the rest of the world is a jungle'. It was not King Leopold II who said this at the time of the Congo Free State. Nor does it come from the silver-spoon youths of the Flemish far-right Schild & Vrienden who harass young campers at music festivals with their racist chants, such as 'The Congo is Ours'. No. It was a man of standing, a man of power, who made this jungle remark. It was, more specifically, the European Union's rather lethargic foreign policy chief, Señor Josep Borrell. He is also in charge of the European diplomatic corps.

On Thursday, 13 October 2022, Borrell addressed the European Diplomatic Academy in Bruges, which was training a new generation of diplomats. Borrell wanted to motivate the novices to go to 'the jungle'; otherwise, 'the jungle could invade the garden.'[1] In contrast to the wilderness of the jungle, the garden is an oasis of peace and civilisation: Josep Borrell was not particularly creative with his metaphor. His address to the would-be diplomats was borrowed from the British colonial empire.

The story goes that in the sixteenth century, British aristocrats began planting vast lawns around their castles. Large tracts of land that were neither farmed nor grazed, just short grass, were unheard of. It is unproductive and extremely expensive, requiring an army of servants to cut and maintain acres of lawn long before the advent of the lawnmower. But it is they, the aristocrats, and they alone, who can afford it. Lawns became a status symbol, and the British took them around the world. The British imperialists boasted that the sun never sets on the British Empire. And where it did set, it would be on their finely cut lawns.

Innovations in architecture and landscaping converged in the construction of the Taj Mahal during India's golden seventeenth century under the Mughal Empire. The garden of the mausoleum depicted the four rivers of Paradise. But the British razed the lush rose bushes, daffodils, and fruit trees to make way for rolling lawns. Acres of lawns also surrounded colonial mansions, from what was to become Sri Lanka to South Africa. So the colonialists felt 'at home'. Jungle is chaos, and finely cut grass is colonial order. So much for Borrell's metaphor.

Señor Borrell's remarks were met with dismay in the Global South. In the European Parliament, Marc Botenga of the Workers' Party of Belgium (PTB-PVDA) called for the statement to be put on the agenda. President of the European Parliament, Roberta Metsola, frowned as Marc spoke.

'Dear colleagues, what's the difference between a garden and a jungle? A garden is a nice place where civilised human beings

1 Josep Borrell, 'European Diplomatic Academy: Opening remarks by High Representative Josep Borrell at the inauguration of the pilot programme', European Union External Action, 13 October 2022.

walk around. A jungle is the heart of darkness where wild animals live. Now, many people in Africa, Asia, Latin America remember very well how, in the name of civilisation, European colonialism treated them like wild animals, enslaving them, torturing them, and even exhibiting them in human zoos. Therefore, when the highest diplomat of the European Union compares the rest of the world, to a jungle, we cannot let that message pass.'

The intervention went viral around the world. Marc's video has been viewed 5.9 million times on the *Middle East Eye* news website alone.

FIVE WATERSHED MOMENTS

It's difficult for some old-world leaders to grasp that new world relations are emerging. Their neo-colonial mindset is deeply embedded, and anyone pointing this out to them faces the wrath of anti-wokeism. Then the gentlemen indulge in aggrieved reverse victimisation: 'They even want to take away our traditions!'. Like the seventh Duchess of Bedford, their world view is that of a neat and tidy lawn with tea at four.

But that's not the rest of the planet's worldview. Voices are rising everywhere for fair trade and true democracy. In the South, most countries have no appetite for another round of superpower competition, the US-China geopolitical tug-of-war. They don't want to be straitjacketed by, 'If you're not with us, you're against us'. High-minded lessons about the right and wrong sides of history no longer impress them. Indeed, they have some of their own history to tell.

In July 2023, several Latin American and Caribbean heads of government spent several days as guests in the heart of Brussels for a summit with the European Union. In 2011, Latin Americans and Caribbeans organised themselves in CELAC, the Community of 33 Latin American and Caribbean States. This cooperation can rightly be described as historic, as it was the first time that multilateral cooperation had been initiated in this region without interference from the United States. At the Brussels summit in 2023, Latin America, the Caribbean, and the European Union were trying to reach a framework agreement for mutual relations, fair trade, and respect. They had their work cut out because the preachy and hegemonic attitude of some EU member states is never far away. Speaking ahead of the summit, a senior European Union diplomat tells *Euronews*: 'It looks like they want to be perceived as equal partners'.[2] You might want to re-read this sentence: it 'seems' that they 'want to be seen' as 'equal partners'. In that European diplomat's mind, countries from Latin America and the Caribbean are not equal partners.

As the world changes, some people's thinking stagnates. Some diplomats, leaders and forces in Europe have not wanted to see the breaking points of recent history. The illegal war in Iraq in 2003, the global financial crisis of 2008, the Copenhagen climate summit in 2009, the pandemic in 2020, and the war in Ukraine in 2022 have changed the landscape for the United States. Washington has become vulnerable, and more and more countries are exploring alternatives. Let's take a brief look at the five watershed moments in this process.

(1) 2003

'Our nation is chosen by God. . . to be a model to the world'. This is what George W. Bush announced to the world in the summer of the year 2000. He was governor of Texas at the time and in the running for president of the United States. Shortly afterwards, the Almighty himself or, rather, his earthly envoy, George W. Bush, takes up residence in the White House. 'Either you are with us, or

2 Aida Sanchez Alonso, 'Ukraine set to haunt EU summit with Latin American countries as it looks to tie up trade links', *Euronews.com*, 14 July 2023.

you are with the terrorists', Bush declared after two planes crashed
into the World Trade Center in the financial district of Manhattan
in New York. The date was 11 September 2001, now referred to
as 'nine eleven' for short. Bush responded to the terrorist attack
by sending bombers to Afghanistan, launching his War on Terror.

In the early 1990s, Afghan mujahideen guerrillas formed
a new organisation: the Taliban. Washington had armed and
trained many of its fighters to counter the Soviet invasion of
Afghanistan in the first half of the 1980s. However, by providing
military assistance, the United States opened Pandora's box. The
first to suffer from the Taliban's extremism were the countries
surrounding Afghanistan. As the Taliban continued to gain
ground in Pakistan and Afghanistan in the second half of the
1990s, China, Kazakhstan, Kyrgyzstan, Russia, Tajikistan, and later
Uzbekistan put their heads together to see what could be done to
ensure regional security. This cooperation led, in June 2001, to
the creation of the Shanghai Cooperation Organisation (SCO),
now the largest regional organisation in the world. It never even
occurred to George W. Bush in 2001 to consult the SCO about his
self-willed crusade.

In March 2003, a Pentagon-led alliance engineered an illegal
war on Iraq. On the pretext that the country had weapons of mass
destruction – which later turned out to be a lie – the West invaded
Iraq. The conquerors dismantled all the government institutions
in place and the army. A major sectarian struggle emerged from
this power vacuum in the country. Millions of people were
displaced, cities like Fallujah were bombed to the ground, and
much of southern Iraq was contaminated with depleted uranium
munitions. New extremist organisations, such as the terrorist
group Islamic State (ISIS), begin to thrive on the sick soil of war.

Since the invasion of Iraq, there has been no end in sight to
the War on Terror. God's chosen model for Bush is as belligerent
as they come and has not made the world a safer place. In fact,
a report by the Watson Institute in May 2023 documents the

catastrophic situation created by the war on terror waged by the United States and its allies. The report is entitled *How Death Outlives War*.[3] In Afghanistan, Iraq, Pakistan, Syria, Yemen, Libya, and Somalia alone, at least 4.5 million people have lost their lives. Millions have been killed, not by acts of war but by their aftermath. The wars have led to economic collapse, destroying medical infrastructure and public services, and making food insecurity and impoverishment the norm. According to the Watson Institute, children have suffered the most.

The US-led War on Terror has destroyed the Fertile Crescent, the rich soils of Mesopotamia, from the Persian Gulf through the Euphrates and Tigris rivers to the shores of the Levantine Sea. Although not always obvious in the metropolises of the North, the watershed moment of 2003 is engraved in everyone's memory in the Global South. As Fiona Hill, a US security specialist, said:

'The U.S. invasion of Iraq universally undercut US credibility and continues to do so. For many critics of the United States, Iraq was the most recent in a series of American sins stretching back to Vietnam.'[4]

What is clear: 2003 is a breaking point.

(2) 2008

The second watershed moment is the global financial crisis of 2007-2008. The crisis is a shock for large emerging countries such as India and China, which have put many of their eggs in the Western growth basket. With the sudden collapse of the Wall Street financial system, it is becoming clear that the US economy will not remain the 'last resort' forever. The crisis has eroded

3 Watson Institute, 'How Death Outlives War: The Reverberating Impact of the Post-9/11 Wars on Human Health', 15 May 2023.
4 Lennart Meri Lecture 2023 by Fiona Hill. LMC, May 2023.

the credibility of Western financial institutions. In response, five major emerging countries band together to become a new player on the world stage: Brazil, Russia, India, China and South Africa, an alliance that comes to be known by the acronym BRICS.

Changing the global financial system was the greatest common denominator, bringing the BRICS countries together. They criticised Wall Street for causing the financial crash of 2008 and making the global community suffer the consequences. They discussed how the United Nations can be reformed into a democratic body without the omnipotence of the Security Council. They began to work on an alternative to the dollar-based financial system.

For the five emerging countries, the international system was not only failing financially but also failing when it came to major challenges such as fair world trade, commodity management, ecological transition, and peace. The alliance was born out of the search for a just alternative – politically, economically, and financially.

(3) 2009

The Copenhagen Climate Summit in December 2009, a year after the financial crisis, marks the third watershed moment. The summit was a flop. Copenhagen was dubbed 'Nopenhagen' in the headlines. On the tenth day of the talks, negotiators from the Group of 77 – 134 countries from the Global South – left the conference centre. They were led by the African delegations. 'They are trying to kill Kyoto', said Lumumba Di-Aping, Sudan's chief negotiator for the Group of 77.[5] This is an extremely sensitive topic, and for good reason. The 1997 Kyoto Protocol recognises common but differentiated responsibilities for global warming (building on the Rio Summit of 1992). A major historical responsibility for

5 Natalie Eggermont, *Climate Express. Sporen van verandering*, EPO, Berchem, 2015, p.97.

greenhouse gas emissions lies with the European countries, Japan, and the United States. Industrialised nations were able to develop and conquer the world by burning fossil fuels. The countries whose wealth was built on colonisation represent barely 14 per cent of the world's population but are responsible for more than 70 per cent of greenhouse gas emissions.

Without a large increase in energy use, development in the South is not possible in any scenario. The Kyoto Protocol explicitly states that the South is also entitled to a share of the emissions so that it can develop.

The first victims of climate change are blameless. Residents of small island states, fishermen in low-lying coastal areas of Bangladesh, and poor farmers in the Philippines and Mozambique are faced with more severe tropical storms. Generally, the poorest are hardest hit by the climate crisis.[6] It goes without saying that the countries of the South have been demanding fair compensation for years. This would allow them to curb their own emissions and adapt to the impacts of global warming.

At the Copenhagen summit, the rich countries pledged $100 billion a year in climate funding by 2020. The money was supposed to help countries of the South adapt to climate change. Little has happened with the fund to date.[7] Yet, it is crucial. The South also needs to be able to finance alternative development models using renewable energy. With high levels of debt and soaring interest rates, there is no money now left to invest in expensive green technology.[8] What's more, some creditors are demanding commodities as collateral for their loans. Poor countries' loans can then be repaid in the form of oil, coal, or gas, if need be. But this

6 Marina Romanello, 'The 2022 report of the Lancet Countdown on health and climate change: health at the mercy of fossil fuels', *The Lancet*, volume 400, issue 10363, pp.1619-1654, 5 November 2022.

7 Jocelyn Timperley, 'The broken $100-billion promise of climate finance and how to fix it', *Nature*, 20 October 2021.

8 Tess Woolfenden, 'The debt-fossil fuel trap. Why debt is a barrier to fossil fuel phase-out and what we can do about it', *Debt Justice*, July 2023.

keeps developing countries shackled to the fossil fuel industry.[9] Talk of *carbon colonialism* is also on the rise. The term comes from the Sixth Assessment Report of the international climate scientists on the IPCC.[10] Carbon colonialism outsources the production of green energy to poor countries on the same scale as old colonialism: multinationals produce where raw materials and labour are cheapest and where they have unlimited access to land. They add up their profits later at the headquarters.

German-British Hyphen, for instance, controls four thousand square kilometres in Namibia to develop green hydrogen projects from solar energy.[11] The plan is to supply it to Germany, Namibia's former coloniser. The Belgian government also wants to establish a 'liquid sun in the form of green hydrogen' project like this in Namibia, Prime Minister De Croo and Energy Minister Van der Straeten enthusiastically announced.[12] But what do the Namibians get out of it all? The Belgian government's press release makes no mention of this.[13] And yet, almost half of Namibia's population has no access to electricity and has to make do with oil lamps. The country has to import a third of its energy needs from neighbouring South Africa.[14] And now it's going to serve as a cheap source of green energy for Germany and Belgium?!

Technology and infrastructure will play a crucial role in the climate transition. It's unacceptable that large companies based in the North are using the latest and best green technologies produced with commodities from the South or even at production sites in the South while denying the South the use of that knowledge.

9 Ibid.

10 Priyadarshi R. Shukla et al., 'Climate Change 2022. Mitigation of Climate Change', Intergovernmental Panel on Climate Change, 2022, p.454.

11 *Hyphen*, 'Southern Corridor Development Initiative (SCDI) Namibian Green Hydrogen Project', hyphenafrica.com.

12 Alexander De Croo, 'Groene waterstof: België toont troeven en ambities aan Namibië', *premier.be*, 16 February 2022.

13 Ibid.

14 Reuters, 'Africa's first hydrogen power plant to produce electricity by 2024', *Al Jazeera*, 12 September 2022.

For all the fine words about technology transfer, the patent system continues to keep them from having to share new developments. The United Nations warns that going green will only widen the global gap between rich and poor.[15]

(4) 2020

As we entered 2020, a microscopic thingamajig, COVID-19, spread across the planet at lightning speed with total disregard for borders. Yet the response to COVID-19 was to erect walls. The Big Pharma of the West refused to lift the vaccine patents. This is the fourth watershed moment. 'While the West kept saying we were all in this together, the world watched as Western countries monopolised vaccines', confirmed Professor Len Ishmael.[16] That left its mark. So, it's only logical that countries of the South began to forge more mutual relations and that South–South cooperation rose.

This was not the first time that the West monopolised vaccines. My last book, *They Have Forgotten Us*, tells the story of the AIDS epidemic at the end of the last century:

'For three decades, the pharmaceutical industry had lobbied hard to secure its intellectual property rights internationally. In 1994, it succeeded with the TRIPS Agreement. The repercussions for the countries of the South were severe. HIV treatment costs $10,000 per patient per year, and the new agreement closed the door on cheaper generics.'[17]

15 United Nations Conference on Trade and Development, 'Green technologies: Coherent policy action needed for developing countries to reap the benefits', Unctad.org, 16 March 2023.

16 Véronique Kiesel, 'Len Ishmael: Puisque l'Occident assure d'abord ses propres intérêts, le Sud global fait désormais la même chose', *Le Soir*, 22 May 2023.

17 Peter Mertens, *They Have Forgotten Us. The Working Class, Care and the Looming Crisis*, New Delhi: LeftWord Books, 2020, pp.90-91.

Five million South Africans were infected, and the situation in Brazil was equally dramatic. Both countries were in urgent need of affordable drugs to treat millions of people. India, one of the largest producers of these drugs at the time, was unable to supply cheap or generic drugs because of the World Trade Organisation's strict intellectual property laws. Eventually, President Nelson Mandela went on the offensive, issuing compulsory licences that allowed generic HIV drugs to enter the country. A lesser-known fact is that in the wake of the AIDS crisis, representatives from India, Brazil, and South Africa met to discuss the issue of medication, health and intellectual property. The group called itself IBSA, after the three countries' first letters. This cooperation in 2003 was something of a precursor to the BRICS initiative that came six years later.

What's more, the COVID pandemic drove public debt to record levels in almost every country. By the end of 2022, it was nine trillion dollars. The poorest countries had to shell out more and more money to satisfy their creditors. And these extra charges came at the expense of hospitals, schools, and infrastructure. This is how they lost public wealth. As many as 60 countries began to spend more on interest payments than on healthcare. It's a staggering observation.

According to the United Nations, more than 50 countries in the South became at increased risk of debt distress. Like Zambia, Mali, and Suriname, Sri Lanka has succumbed to spiralling debt. They notice that the West will open its wallet to serve its own interests, but not for them. They don't need knights sitting on their moral high horses coming to lecture other countries.

(5) 2022

On 24 February 2022, Russian armies invaded independent Ukraine. We'll look at that in detail in the next chapter. Most countries condemn the attack as a flagrant violation of international law, and rightly so. The South understands the importance of sovereignty and international law like no other.

But when it comes to imposing sanctions, there is much less of an appetite. The research team at *The Economist* has calculated that only 52 countries comprising 15 per cent of the global population support and implement the sanctions. Far fewer put themselves squarely behind Russia: a mere 12. The research institution's decision is clear: 'some 127 states are categorised as not being clearly in either camp'.[18]

The West, accustomed to centuries of domination, is astonished to discover that neither carrots nor sticks can discipline the countries of the Global South. Geopolitics expert Martin Quencez explains:

'It shows they feel comfortable enough to openly oppose the West.

'The former power of Washington and European capitals to keep Global South countries in line has diminished sharply. The vote confronted the fact that these swing states are going their own way. Countries like Brazil and India put their national interests first, such as securing energy and food imports.'[19]

The perception that the West has double standards is almost universal in the South. It holds especially true for the US. This happened during the Cold War when Washington backed ruthless autocrats like Chiang Kai-shek of Taiwan, Muhammad Reza Pahlavi of Iran, Syngman Rhee of South Korea, Mobutu Sese Seko of Zaire, Anastasio Somoza of Nicaragua, and Augusto Pinochet of Chile, to name but a few. And today is no different. Palestinian

---

18 *The Economist*, 'How to survive a superpower split', 11 April 2023.
19 Erik Ziarczyk, 'Oorlog in Oekraïne legt fundamenten multipolaire wereldorde bloot'. *De Tijd*, 23 May 2023, pp.6-7.

resistance to the brutal Israeli occupation is not supported. Instead, it's the Israeli army that's equipped with military hardware.

The Antwerp police are leaving for a working visit to the Israeli police, as I write this, under the leadership of Mayor Bart De Wever. It comes barely two weeks after the Israeli army's biggest incursion into the West Bank in two decades. No one in Belgium's traditional political families cares any longer. Seventy-five years of apartheid, seventy-five years of international law violations: it all seems to have been normalised. And Cuba has been besieged for sixty years with the most unlikely of sanctions and an illegal blockade designed to strangle it financially and economically, simply because the tiny island committed the crime of wanting to be sovereign.

Two Weights, Two Measures

'History is sometimes full of irony', says Craig Mokhiber. The US lawyer is a specialist in international human rights policy. After having been a UN human rights official for thirty-one years, he resigned from his post, frustrated by the international response to the war of destruction against Palestine. He says,

> "This year marks the 75th anniversary of the Universal Declaration of Human Rights, the cornerstone of the human rights movement around the world. But 1948 was also the year of the Nakba in Palestine, the year 450 Palestinian villages were destroyed, and 750,000 Palestinians were expelled from their territory. It was also the year South Africa introduced apartheid'.

Mokhiber is right. The year of the Universal Declaration of Human Rights was also the birth year of the Palestinian catastrophe and South African apartheid. After a long and sustained struggle, also involving the international community, apartheid was finally abolished in South Africa. That struggle shaped my young consciousness. When I was seventeen, we sold 'Boycott Apartheid' badges to the cinemas where *Cry Freedom* about Steve Biko was being shown. Almost everyone agreed at the time: apartheid laws were an affront to international law and universal human rights.

However, a different standard has always been applied to Palestine. The expulsion of the Palestinians in 1948 violated Article 2 of the United Nations Charter. Although this was not in doubt, no one imposed sanctions. In 1967, following its illegal conquest of the West Bank, Israel established an apartheid regime with separate military laws for the Palestinian population and civil laws for the Jewish settlers. The United Nations demanded that Israel withdraw its troops. But nothing happened: no sanctions, no prosecution, no intervention. In 1980, the United Nations passed Resolution 465, demanding that Israel dismantle all of its illegal settlements. Once again, nothing happened. And every time someone wanted to do something, the United States vetoed it.

Countries in the South have long been aware of the West's double standards and that the White House is the final arbiter of what will or will not happen.

A month after Russia's illegal invasion of Ukraine, the International Criminal Court in The Hague issued an arrest warrant against Russian President Putin for the forced relocation of six thousand children. In the first month of Israel's war on Gaza, over five thousand children have been killed. But we have yet to see a serious investigation by the same International Criminal Court, let alone a warrant to arrest Israeli Prime Minister Netanyahu. As the UNICEF spokesperson said,

'Gaza has become a graveyard for thousands of children and a living hell for everyone else.'

An economic and military embargo was imposed on Moscow immediately after the Russian invasion of Ukraine. Yet there is not the barest economic or military embargo against Israel. The European Union maintains the EU-Israel Association Agreement, affording Israelis full access to European technology, science, and universities. And the United States is supplying the bombs and weapons used to bombard Gaza into the Middle Ages. The US-Israeli axis of war believes that it is above all laws and that it can and will get away with anything. However, this axis is more isolated than ever. Cuba has made that clear. In a United Nations General Assembly vote in November 2023, 187 countries voted unanimously to lift the blockade of Cuba. Only two countries voted against it: the United States and Israel. Of all the countries in the world, the US could only get Israel on its side against Cuba. Washington's only ally is the apartheid state, which has imposed an illegal blockade on Gaza for years. What moral authority can come out of these two voices?

The United States has been at war with Cuba for sixty years, imposing the longest blockade in modern history. This blockade is illegal, immoral, and criminal. Not only is it a blockade against an independent country, but it is also a blockade against a proud people defending their sovereignty. And it is also a blockade by which the United States tries by any means to diminish a socialist ideal.

You cannot be sovereign and continue to listen to Washington's ukases. Every country that claims sovereignty should establish its own relations, not submit to the illegal, coercive and punitive practices of the United States.

Double Mutiny

Tu nos dices que debemos sentarnos
Pero las ideas solo pueden levantarnos
Caminar, recorrer, no rendirse ni retroceder
You tell us to sit down,
but ideas only make us stand up,
walk, march – not surrender nor retreat.
Shadia Mansour and Ana Tijoux, *Somos Sur*

London's new tube line means it's easy to get to Southall Station now. Harsev Bains, who was born in Punjab and grew up in Leicester, is waiting for me there. Pointing to the jewellery, trinkets, and antiques in the colourful shops, he smiles and asks if I need anything to take home. Because so many Indians have lived here since the 1950s, Southall in west London is known as *Little Punjab*. On our way to Southall Town Hall, we pass restaurant after restaurant serving samosas, dosas, and sweets like jalebis.

Harsev Bains works in the aircraft industry. He is a trade union organiser and a spokesman for the Indian Workers' Association – the largest Indian labour association in the United Kingdom. Harsev continues to follow political developments in his native country closely. He exclaims,

'Three crucial elections are coming up in 2024: in the US, the UK and in India.'

When he omits the elections in tiny Belgium, I ignore it. Because Harsev is anxious and not without reason. He continues,

'Narendra Modi, the prime minister of India, had three key friends: Donald Trump in the US, Jair Bolsonaro in Brazil, and Boris Johnson here in the UK. He has lost all three. But his domestic policies are no less right-wing for it. You know Peter, Modi is doing everything he can to secure a third term next year. That's the worst thing that could happen. Fortunately, 26 opposition parties have formed an alliance against Modi. But it's not going to be easy'.

Things are on the move in India. And India is huge. At the end of August, the country became the first to land on the moon's south pole. And a space mission of its own is underway to study the sun. No country can do this without enormous effort or technological prowess. India is now the world's third-largest economy after China and the United States. Meanwhile, divisions have widened, especially since the right-wing Hindu nationalist Indian People's Party, the Bharatiya Janata Party (BJP), came to power in 2014. Almost nowhere else in the world are exorbitant wealth and abject poverty so closely intertwined: the social divide is enormous. One in five people in India is poor. And the ruling BJP is also doing all it can to stir up religious dissent. Harsev tells me,

'In Modi's BJP circles, they even want to make Mahatma Gandhi's assassin a saint'.

One of the leaders of the Indian independence movement against the British, Gandhi advocated a secular policy away from any religious extremism. Harsev adds,

'Gandhi's assassin was a far-right militant of the Hindu paramilitary organisation Rashtriya Swayamsevak Sangh (RSS). This type of person now calls the shots. We're seeing more and more religious minorities, especially Muslims, targeted'.

Harsev stirs his milky tea, clinking his spoon against the cup. He says,

'You know, Peter, on the day India celebrated its 75th anniversary of independence from British rule, the authorities released eleven rapists who had been sentenced to life imprisonment for gang rape and murder'.

In 2002, anti-Muslim pogroms in the western state of Gujarat resulted in the deaths of more than 2,000 people, most of them Muslims. Hundreds of women were raped. Narendra Modi was then chief minister of the state.

'Even then, he was under fire for not doing enough to stop the killings and for shielding the perpetrators'.

Eleven men were ultimately sentenced to life imprisonment. Now they have been released. Instead of a day of celebration, #IndiaAt75 became a day of shame.

~~~

'But it's not all doom and gloom,' Harsev assures me:

'Resistance does exist. You know what happened to the farmers, right?'

I hesitate. Harsev takes this as an invitation to continue.

'For 388 days, farmers fought Modi's laws to liberalise agriculture. And in the end, they won. After a year of action and 741 deaths, the government was forced to announce that it would repeal the laws'. 'Do you know how that happened?'.

Harsev is quick to answer his own question:

'The farmers formed a front. They transcended caste. And they united with the workers. Nothing like this had ever really happened before. In November 2020, the strikes involved up to 250 million people. That's half of India's working class. They may well have been the largest general strikes in human history. The United Farmers' Front has proven that even ordinary people can change things if they all work together.'

I suggest,

'So, there's actually a double mutiny going on,' 'Farmers, women, workers, and minorities rebelling against Modi's reactionary government. And at the same time, a kind of mutiny by the Indian government against the current world order.'

Harsev nods,

'It's a complex situation. Internationally, the Indian government is forging its own path. It does business with the Russians in roubles as a way of avoiding sanctions. It trades heavily with China, despite border disputes. In Brazil, Modi used to have to deal with his friend Bolsonaro, but now it's Lula'.

India was already non-aligned during the first Cold War, building relations with both the Soviet Union and the United States. It holds the same independent position again today. During the coronavirus pandemic, India won international acclaim for supplying millions of vaccines not only to neighbouring countries but also to the World Health Organisation. No matter how much the US tries to woo it, the Indian government, however right-wing, will not be easily swayed by Washington.

Vijay Prashad agrees,

'Of course, there is criticism of the activities of the BRICS countries. Look at the Indian government, for instance: it has destroyed democracy, it's persecuting the farmers and so on. But that doesn't mean you don't have a logical understanding of the role of a country like India on the world stage. On the one hand, India is working on a large-scale capitalist project against its own people, and on the other, it is also turning to Western countries and saying: "Your problems are not our problems".'

With this last sentence, Vijay is referring to what India's external affairs minister, Jaishankar, said when he pinpointed the issue:

'Europe has to grow out of the mindset that Europe's problems are the world's problems, but the world's problems are not Europe's problems'.[1]

~ ~ ~

With so much rebellion in the air, voices are also being raised in the United States for a slightly different view of things. Fiona Hill, former National Security Council staffer and veteran of three presidencies, is one of those voices. In early May 2023, Hill warned

'This is a mutiny against what they [the Global South] see as the collective West'.

Concerned, she adds:

1 *The Economist*, 'How to survive a superpower split', 11 April 2023.

'In 2023, we hear a resounding no to US domination and see a marked appetite for a world without a hegemon'.

For Hill, the reaction of the countries of the South to the war in Ukraine is nothing less than 'mutiny', an 'open rebellion', 'a rebellion of the rest against the United States'. The security specialist notes that 'America fatigue' and 'disillusionment with its role as the global hegemon' is widespread.[2]

You just need eyes to see it: across the South, new forms of cooperation are mushrooming. They often colour outside the traditional, expected lines. And the countries involved may differ greatly from one another politically, but when it comes to trade, they can all use the same door. BRICS brings together countries with different political views and sometimes even border disputes. In their dealings and relationships with each other, they keep their feet on the ground, guided by sound pragmatism. Nobody can be blamed for that. US political scientist John Mearsheimer explains:

'States... coexist in a world where there is no supreme authority that can protect them from each other',

When it comes to international relations, he is a man of authority. He soberly observes,

'Survival, of course, is the primary goal of states, because if a state does not survive, it cannot pursue any other goals'.

'This situation forces them to pay close attention to the balance of power, because they understand that being weak can leave them vulnerable. Thus, states compete among themselves for power, which is not to say they do not cooperate when their interests are compatible'.[3]

2 Lennart Meri Lecture 2023 by Fiona Hill. LMC, May 2023. https://lmc.icds. ee/lennart-meri-lecture-by-fiona-hill/
3 John Mearsheimer, 'Pourquoi les grandes puissances se font la guerre', Le

Peel away the thin veneer of morality and emotion, and you will see that a down-to-earth approach has always been the way the Northern countries have built their power, despite often major economic or military disagreements.

Differences of opinion also exist among the BRICS-plus members. Brazil has a relatively progressive government team in power, while India has a reactionary government at the helm. The differences in wealth and income between the BRICS partners are massive, and some have strong historical border disputes, such as those between India and China. Some questionable former US partners, such as Saudi Arabia, have also joined the BRICS alliance. It's a very mixed bag with many internal contradictions. Anyone expecting the eleven BRICS-plus countries to have a common left-wing agenda can only be disappointed. This is not to say that renewed southern cooperation is unimportant. As the era of a world led by a single pole, the United States, quietly fades away, the Global South is re-emerging. And it is doing so with the parallel movement that has always existed.

There is the power from below, with grassroots movements trying to push through a progressive agenda. Each doing so in their own context, from the landless rural workers' movement, MST, in Brazil and the great women's movement, All India Democratic Women's Association, in India, to the struggle of the metalworkers' union, NUMSA, in South Africa. It's a mutiny below deck, a vocal call for democratic rights, land reform and decently paid work. It is also the struggle for freedom against reactionary and dictatorial regimes that deserves our support. And then, above deck too, the Global South is in turmoil, searching for a new form of non-alignment, a realpolitik that serves national interests.

That is the double mutiny at play.

Bazazo and the Dollar

Master of these politics, you swear that you got options (slave,
yeah)
Master of opinion 'cause you vote with the white collar (slave)
The Thirteenth Amendment says that slavery's abolished (shit)
Look at all these slave masters posin' on yo' dollar (get it)
  Run The Jewels, JU$T

His first shop was small. But he had to do something to make
ends meet and support his family. In 1986, Moheidein Bazazo
was in high spirits when he opened his mini market in civil war-
ravaged Beirut. And it was a success. More and more people came
to good-humoured Moheidein's shop to do their weekly shopping.
Just a few years later, he had shelves full of food and needed a staff
of twelve to run his bustling business. Who would have thought
it possible? But those days are gone. Now, Bazazo works mostly
alone, often in the dark, to reduce his electricity bill. His regulars
struggle to make ends meet, and when they buy less, he buys less,
leaving shelves and fridges empty. He's alone in his shop every
morning, restocking shelves but mostly adjusting prices to the
day's inflation.

The Lebanese pound has crashed. In 2019, you paid 1,500
pounds for one dollar. Today, you officially have to pay 15,000 for
the same dollar. That's the theory because, in practice, there's so
much mistrust of the Lebanese currency that a dollar is usually
exchanged for 80,000 Lebanese pounds. Prices change almost
hourly, but it's hard to change the price tag on a sack of flour or rice
every hour. That's madness. So Bazazo decided he had no option
but to list his prices in dollars. He no longer takes Lebanese pounds,

only US dollars. It's a reluctant decision. But he has no choice if he does not want to go bankrupt. For many of his customers, it's a disaster. Lebanese are paid in Lebanese pounds, and only the wealthiest have access to dollars. As a result, basic goods such as food are becoming unaffordable for many.

The story of Bazazo and his customers mirrors that of many in the South. Ecuador and Zimbabwe were also forced to switch to the dollar as their own currencies plummeted. That's hyperinflation: you need thicker and thicker wads of money to buy the same sack of flour or rice. In such situations, countries naturally resort to the US dollar as a form of payment, a practice that has been in place since the end of the Second World War.

Bretton Woods

But how did the dollar become the currency of world trade? That's a fair question because about 80 per cent of world trade is conducted in green dollar bills. Oil, grain, steel, copper, and other commodities are traded in dollars. This means that even trade between two countries that have nothing to do with the United States is still conducted in US dollars. But why? The greenback's status as an international currency seems to be a law of nature. As if it had always been so and could not be otherwise.

The dollar is not only the world's preeminent trading currency but also its reserve currency. Is a reserve currency something like a substitute bench in football, ready to step in when needed? Yes and no. Yes, because the reserve currency is used when the domestic currency loses significant value. And no, because the reserve currency is often the better currency, better than the domestic currency, while the substitute bench in football is usually not as good as the team on the pitch.

Here's how it works: countries have financial reserves used to invest or pay international bills. They hold part of their reserves in foreign currencies rather than in their own currency. This reserve currency is considered safe. It provides confidence that countries will meet their external obligations. The reserve currency is like secure collateral. Today, over 60 per cent of global national reserves are held in dollars. The dollar is seen as a safe haven, but only the US Federal Reserve can print dollars.

Would it not then be better to use a different international currency as a means of payment? This was, in fact, an option at the end of the Second World War. For this, we have to travel to the northeast of the United States, to the town of Carroll in New Hampshire. Carroll has just under a thousand inhabitants. The town is surrounded by the White Mountain National Forest. The views are phenomenal, with the snow-capped Mount Washington on one side and the Presidential Range on the other. In 1944, delegates from 44 allied nations gathered there at the stately Mount Washington Hotel on the grounds known as Bretton Woods. Although there are representatives from Brazil to the Philippines and from Nigeria to New Zealand, the conference has not been set up as a democratic global event. Two rival powers, the United States and Britain, are doing all the talking. Economist Harry Dexter White is the key figure in the US delegation. Economist John Maynard Keynes is among the delegates from the United Kingdom. They would rather not see other countries get a finger in the pie.

The talk at Bretton Woods is all about rebuilding Europe, not rebuilding colonial countries after the plunder of colonialism. Keynes complains when a wary voice touches on the subject now and again. The British economist writes a letter to London from his hotel lobby, stating that the countries of the South 'clearly have nothing to contribute' to the conference. He grumbles that with all these delegations, the conference is 'the most monstrous monkey-house assembled for years'.[1] The colonial spirit lingers on. Let countries supplying the raw materials have a say? No, thanks. The two imperial powers, Great Britain and the United States set the rules of the game and prepared the conference thoroughly. Their preparations took two and a half years. It doesn't even cross their mind to let other countries have a say, let alone the countries of the South.

However, the British are also going to have a rude awakening because the specific weight of the United States is decisive. The United States' allies are economically depleted by the war; they

1 Vijay Prashad, *The Darker Nations*. o.c., p. 68.

need US aid to survive. Washington can thus have its way. Britain may have dominated the world in the nineteenth century, but it's now the United States' turn to wield the global sceptre. That's the outcome of the conference. As the British business newspaper *Financial Times* later noted,

'One of the reasons Bretton Woods worked was that the US was clearly the most powerful country at the table, and so ultimately was able to impose its will on the others, including an often-dismayed Britain'.

Followed by:

'At the time, one senior official at the Bank of England described the deal reached at Bretton Woods as "the greatest blow to Britain next to the war", largely because it underlined the way in which financial power had moved from the UK to the US'.[2]

The two superpowers at Bretton Woods agree: the financial crisis of the 1930s helped precipitate the Second World War. Experience has taught us that economic wars can turn into military wars. Harry Dexter White, the architect of the agreements, articulated it this way:

'The absence of a high degree of economic collaboration among the leading nations will... inevitably result in economic warfare that will be a prelude and instigator of military warfare on an even vaster scale'.

These words from 1945 are more relevant today than ever. The task at the Mount Washington Hotel in Bretton Woods

2 Gideon Rachman, 'The Bretton Woods sequel will flop', *Financial Times*, 10 November 2008.

was clear: to establish a new financial system to facilitate global trade. It requires a widely accepted means of investing, trading, and paying. They opted for a system of fixed exchange rates so that the value of one currency was pegged to the value of another currency, or a basket of other currencies, or gold. Such a system makes trading with each other easier and more predictable. And it's designed to prevent sudden and abrupt devaluations and to discourage speculation. A new institution, the International Monetary Fund, was set up as the watchdog.

Keynes proposes creating a new world reserve currency, the *bancor*. It would serve as a means of payment for trade between countries. It would also be safe and secure because the bancor would always be redeemable for gold. Washington torpedoed the idea. A new currency was out of the question. After all, was it not true that the United States controlled two-thirds of the world's gold? The international trading currency, they insisted, must and will be the dollar, backed by gold. Washington got its way, promising to exchange every dollar for a fixed amount of gold. From then on, the dollar was pegged to the gold standard: one ounce of gold, exactly 28.3495231 grams, cost $35. And so, the dollar became the world trade currency.

~~~

United States intervention in the Vietnam War cost Washington dearly in the 1960s. The United States also had to contend with high domestic inflation: goods were becoming increasingly expensive. The Federal Reserve the US central bank, printed new dollar notes, but they became worth less and less. By 1971, money supply growth was at 10 per cent. For the same amount of goods, 10 per cent more money was available. Not so safe after all, thought more and more countries, as they began to exchange their dollars for gold.

Gold coverage of US bank notes fell from 55 per cent to 22

per cent: barely one-fifth of the greenbacks could still be redeemed for gold. Washington grew nervous. Would there be a run on the dollar? Washington would be short of this precious metal if all countries wanted to convert their dollars into gold. It would be a huge problem. President Richard Nixon issued Executive Order 11615 on 15 August 1971 to avert a crisis. The convertibility of the dollar into gold ended with this order. The dollar was no longer backed by gold.

The United States had already got its way at Bretton Woods, but there had been some negotiation. By contrast, the death knell of the Bretton Woods agreements was a unilateral decree from Washington devoid of any consultation with the international community. This came to be dubbed 'the Nixon Shock'. Fixed exchange rates were also abandoned two years later. From then on, they floated. The price of the dollar was no longer stable. It could fluctuate wildly depending on market supply, demand, and speculation, precisely what they had tried to prevent at Bretton Woods. However, none of this meant the end of dollar dominance because oil replaced gold as collateral. In 1979, the US government agreed with Saudi Arabia to sell oil only in dollars. In return, the Saudis received a steady supply of weapons and the promise of a stable dollar. This deal marked the birth of the petrodollar: if countries wanted to import oil, they needed US dollars. Obviously, they were unable to print it themselves. How were they supposed to get dollars? The solution was simple: export enough goods and commodities to the United States in exchange for dollars. By the end of the Second World War, the dollar was the king of world trade; by the 1970s, it was the undisputed emperor.

To this day, the Federal Reserve issues a dual-status currency: national status in the US itself and international status as the leading global reference currency. The armed forces are the military fist, the dollar the economic fist of US dominance. With no gold supply to counterbalance it, the Federal Reserve can effectively print as many dollars as it wants. The only constraint is a political appointment in the United States itself: Congress sets a cap, and a congressional consensus occasionally raises it. Washington decides how many dollars it will print. That affects not just the US economy but also the entire global economy. Although a $100 bill costs about 17 cents to produce, other countries have to put in $100 worth of goods.

Wall Street's criteria have become the world's criteria. Because when things go wrong somewhere, people are forced to turn to the dollar. Moheidein Bazazo and his customers in Lebanon know all about that.

Game Changer

The footprints of those who walk together are never erased.
African proverb

April 2023. 'We won't have to talk about sanctions in five years because there will be so many countries transacting in currencies other than the dollar that we won't have the ability to sanction them', says US Senator Marco Rubio on Fox News.[1] It's as though he is sounding the death knell for dollar hegemony. The images travel around the world.

Countries are groaning under the irresponsible monetary policy of the United States. Constantly raising interest rates makes the dollar more expensive and loans unaffordable. No wonder there is growing discontent and anger at dollar hegemony. However, people like Marco Rubio are not interested in these issues. They lie awake because of something entirely different: how to ensure that Washington does not lose its ability to use unilateral sanctions and coercion. There's a whiff of panic in Rubio's words. This is also a sign of the times.

Washington has never shied away from playing its dollar dominance geopolitically. Economic reprisals followed when the US military was forced to leave Afghanistan in the summer of 2021 after a failed twenty-year war. Afghanistan's dollar reserves were blocked. As a result, Kabul no longer had access to much of its own financial reserves. That's how to bring a country to its

1 4 April 2023
https://twitter.com/IndoPac_Info/status/1643066293359366146?t=-4tLtPGKaW0OkMgwwqS89g&s=09

knees economically. 'The US has been extremely trigger-happy with stinging economic measures', says Gal Luft, the co-director of the Institute for the Analysis of Global Security. Luft refers to 'unacceptable and unheard-of steps' in recent weeks, such as effectively freezing Russia's central bank reserves and disconnecting Russia from the SWIFT interbank messaging system. SWIFT handles communication for international payments between banks. If a bank is isolated from this network, the transfer of payment orders stops, and the bank pretty much collapses.

According to Luft, one in ten countries in the world is under some form of US sanctions. The Washington think tank's director explains that central banks everywhere are wondering if reliance on the dollar and 'putting all their eggs in one basket' is a smart idea.[2] Awareness is growing that it is better not to rely too much on Western financial payment systems. Because on a bad day, you can be barred, too.

Several countries are reducing their dollar reserves and looking for alternatives. Russia and China have already set up their own payment systems. For example, cooperation in trading in local currencies is also on the rise among members of the vast Shanghai Cooperation Organisation. Bangladesh and Iraq now organise some of their trade in the Chinese yuan, while the United Arab Emirates and India close deals in dirhams and rupees. In December 2022, Saudi Arabia conducted its first oil transaction in yuan. Across the ocean, Brazil and Argentina are working on a common currency. The push to *de-dollarise* the world is strong. However, no currency can replace the dollar in the short term. Trade volumes and reserves may shift, but no currency today is as widely redeemable as the dollar. You cannot use the yuan, rupee, or real currency in most global transactions. Most commodities are still traded in dollars. That's why some countries are considering an

---

2 Abigail Ng, 'Washington's trigger-happy sanctions may push countries away from the dollar, says think tank', *CNBC.com*, 21 March 2022.

alternative, such as putting all their eggs in a basket of coins rather than putting all their eggs in the dollar basket. As the International Monetary Fund warns, 'If dollar dominance comes to an end. . . then the greenback could be felled not by the dollar's main rivals but by a broad group of alternative currencies'.

~~~

The eleven BRICS-plus partners represent 46 per cent of the world's population, but together, they have barely 18 per cent of the votes in the International Monetary Fund. The G7's demographic lightweights, which disproportionately dominate political and financial decision-making, are the mirror image.

Without having had adverse experiences with the International Monetary Fund for decades, it's impossible to understand why the New Development Bank has been created. This is because it wants to lend money not to pay off debts, but to build infrastructure. The president of the New Development Bank is former Brazilian president Dilma Rousseff. She says that countries can borrow from the NDB with no strings attached, without the bank telling them what they can or cannot spend on education or healthcare. As a model, it's worlds apart.

Brazil and China may well go one step further. In March 2023, they decided to abandon the dollar in a bid to boost bilateral trade and financial transactions. They want to transact directly in Brazilian real or Chinese yuan without having first to convert the currency into dollars. Agreements like this put people like Senator Marco Rubio on edge. He warns of the danger that 'these countries are creating a parallel economy completely independent of the US'. What is a nightmare scenario for some is a step towards a more balanced world trade for others.

With growing South-South trade, regional partnerships, and the creation of BRICS, Global South countries can now choose

Chinese, Brazilian, Indian, or Western contracts to build their universities, schools, bridges, and hospitals. This is a game changer in neo-colonial world relations and one many metropolises in the West did not see coming.

Chapter 5

Missed Opportunities

The Granary

Yonder
across wheat-laden Ukraine
across Ukraine's wheat sea
and its coveted summer's gold
are dancing Don Cossacks, Don Cossacks
dancing Gogol gnomes
Gogol gnomes, Gogol gnomes in self-assured sway.
      Paul van Ostaijen, *Woord-jazz op Russies gegeven* (Word jazz with a Russian theme)

Steppe steppe, Ukraine's wheat sea. Paul van Ostaijen's poem uses compelling rhythm. He reportedly wrote it after visiting a Russian cabaret in Berlin. Ukraine's wheat sea – you can say that again! *Chernozem*, literally 'black earth', is the most fertile soil in the world. A quarter of it is in Ukraine. Just about everything thrives in this rich soil. Ukrainian grain has fed people from Norway to Pakistan for five thousand years. Ancient Greeks and Romans, Goths, and Huns all fed their armies with it, and Russian prosperity peaked as early as the eighteenth century on the back of grain exports.

Today, Ukraine is home to 42 million hectares of fertile soil. That's almost a third of the total farmland in the European Union. The *chernozem* produces 64 million tonnes of grain and seeds yearly, making Ukraine one of the world's largest producers of barley, wheat, and sunflower oil.

The end of socialist collectivisation in 1991 brought unprecedented virgin black soil onto the market. Oceans of undulating wheat are a tasty morsel for banks and multinationals in the agribusiness sector. Dancing Don Cossacks (oligarchs) from Russia and Ukraine face competition for that morsel from Gogol gnomes (monopolies) in the United States and the European Union.

Since 1991, Ukraine has occupied an intermediate position as a buffer state between East and West. That's what the superpowers agreed. And that's what's written in Ukraine's declaration of independence. But while that's the case on paper, the country is still torn between Moscow, Washington, and Berlin. Meanwhile, in Ukraine, the oligarchs installed a new ruling class. When the Soviet Union collapsed, they became disproportionately rich by looting the public sector. Both East and West wooed the rulers in Kyiv with competing 'aid packages'. Each wanted to draw the world's breadbasket into its own sphere of influence.

In late 2013, tension mounted. A free trade agreement was on the table between the European Union and Ukraine. Viktor Yanukovych, the incumbent president, refused to sign the FTA, but he signed his political death warrant by refusing to do so. In Kyiv's independence square, Maidan Nezalezhnosti, thousands gathered against Yanukovych. The West fuelled the uprising. Amidst the skirmishes, key backroom players kept a cool head. For where there's chaos, there's opportunity. As the Maidan uprising took hold, agribusiness multinational Cargill quietly bought shares in UkrLandFarming for $200 million.[1] Ukrainian billionaire Oleg Bakhmatyuk owned the company. With 670,000 hectares, his firm was the country's most powerful landowner. And it operates in all sectors of the food chain.[2] More than two-thirds of all the calories we eat come from staple foods, especially cereal grains. The average earthling, who obviously doesn't exist, eats one hundred kilograms of cereal grain each year: wheat, rice, or corn. Whoever controls

1   Tim Mullaney, 'For US-Russia, Cold War and corn share long history', *CNBC.com*, 18 March 2014.

2   Ukrainian Grain Association, 'Ukraine: UkrLandFarming to increase its land bank to 670,000 ha.' Uga-port.org, 6 September 2013.

cereal grain controls the gateway to human food. Cargill's CEO knew that, too. In June 2011, Greg Page, that's his name, declared that Ukraine is a 'great place for the world to grow more food'. He added, 'But all the gifts that nature provides can be undone with bad policies'.[3] By bad policies, Cargill's CEO was referring to the land moratorium that Ukraine imposed in 2001 to prevent too much farmland from falling into oligarchical hands. Since then, the moratorium has been a thorn in the side of big Western agribusiness.

The US businesses were not the only ones eyeing the coveted gold wheat sea. As Cargill closed its Ukraine deal, German agribusiness prepared for a meeting with senior Ukrainian officials. Major German firms wanted to do business, they said, but then Ukraine had to 'simplify' its laws.[4] They referred to the tax system, the laws on genetic modification of crops and. . . the land moratorium.

~~~

The February 2014 regime change, the Maidan uprising, was a pivotal moment. In a disconcerting report, the *Oakland Institute* explained the events ten months later.[5] The research institute detailed how international financial institutions capitalised on Ukraine's political upheaval in those weeks to deregulate the country's vast agricultural sector and open it up to foreign companies. The report revealed how companies like Cargill and DuPont continue to take over more and more of Ukraine's agricultural system.

3 Roman Olearchyk, 'Investment key to global food role, Black Sea region told', *Financial Times*, 27 June 2011.

4 Ukrainian Grain Association, 20 German farm companies ready to invest in Ukrainian agriculture. Uga-port.org, 17 January 2014.

5 Jettie Word, Alice Martin-Prevel, and Frederic Mousseau, 'Walking on the West Side: The World Bank and the IMF in the Ukraine Conflict', *Oakland Institute*, 14 December 2014.

After Ukraine's independence in 1991, the government distributed some 30 million hectares of agricultural land to small local farmers. A decade later, it introduced a land moratorium to prevent domestic or foreign oligarchs from acquiring high concentrations of agricultural land. Farmers could only rent or lease their land. As a result, most fertile *chernozem* remained in the hands of small and medium-sized farmers. But they came under pressure and felt the heat. According to a 2019 World Bank report, their land needed to be 'optimised' to create more 'added value'. The aim was to 'accelerate private investment in agriculture'. The liberal rule of international institutions is that small farmers must make way for big agribusiness.

Arms and money poured into Kyiv in the form of aid packages from the World Bank and the International Monetary Fund. But there's no such thing as a free lunch. Ukraine had to make cuts and reform. Agriculture had to be privatised. Not quite seven months after the Maidan uprising, the European Bank for Reconstruction and Development announced that it found ten private agribusinesses willing to invest a billion dollars in Ukrainian agriculture over the next year. But there were strings attached, the bank said, including taxes, import and export laws, and land sales. [6]

Agribusiness giants have operated in Ukraine for some time, but their investments soared after Maidan, primarily in the acquisition of industrial rather than agricultural land. After all, the restrictive laws that apply to agricultural land did not apply to industrial land for processing, storage, and transport. That's why big foreign companies have bought this land. Three of the four major ABCD companies – ADM, Bunge, and Cargill – have invested billions in storage and processing facilities for Ukrainian commodities. They now also claim a larger share of the grain, oilseed, livestock, and feed markets, as well as more storage and

6 European Bank for Reconstruction and Development, EBRD and private sector ready to invest in Ukraine's agribusiness. Ebdr.com, 9 October 2014.

export infrastructure. Cargill owns at least four-grain elevators and at least two processing plants for sunflower oil production in Ukraine. It also acquired a 25 per cent stake in a grain terminal in the Black Sea port of Novorossiysk. The terminal has a capacity of 3.5 million tonnes of grain per year. The world is opening up for Cargill. And Greg Page, the CEO, was jubilant: 'The opportunities in the broader food chain are enormous'.[7]

~ ~ ~

The concentration of agricultural land gradually advanced. The big Ukrainian players knew how to be resourceful with the law: buying up farmland is not allowed, but leasing it is. Meanwhile, large agribusinesses established after 2000 took over more and more of the grain and oilseed production: Kernel, UkrLandFarming, MHP, Agroprosperis, Astarta-Kyiv, and others. Foreign financial players acquired an increasing stake in these large companies.

In 2016, the EU-Ukraine Deep and Comprehensive Free Trade Area, an integral part of the EU–Ukraine Association Agreement, entered into force. European businesses benefited from this. It's a strategic issue for the European Union. Ukraine is part of the European Commission's strategic plan to expand protein crops. The Commission wants parts of agriculture in Ukraine and Eastern Europe to switch to soy, among other crops. The aim? To cease relying on imports from Brazil. The plan was in response to changing global relationships.

In March 2020, the Zelensky government scrapped the land moratorium, in part due to pressure from the International Monetary Fund. Since July 2021, citizens have been able to acquire up to one hundred acres of land each, and from 2024, businesses will also be able to participate in agricultural land auctions. Officially, there's still a ban on sales to foreign companies, but this

---

7 Roman Olearchyk, 'Investment key to global food role, Black Sea region told', *Financial Times*, 27 June 2011.

too could change. The law has been, and remains, particularly controversial in Ukraine. Wheat-laden Ukraine is clearly at the centre of the world's geostrategic chessboard.

Bakhmut

Et après avoir tout vu
Et après avoir tout entendu
Le diable a prononcé un discours:
Ça va, il y a toujours un peu partout
Des feux illuminant la Terre
Ça va, les Hommes s›amusent comme des fous
Au dangereux jeu de la guerre
Having seen all,
having heard all,
the devil gave a speech:
All's well, fires are still everywhere
lighting up the earth.
All's well, men are having the time of their lives
in the dangerous game of war.
     Jacques Brel, *Le Diable* (The Devil)

At the end of March 2021, Nadine and I slip off for a weekend. We want to get some fresh air in Sangatte on the French coast. That's Zandgate in Dutch, a spot where the north wind whistles through your hair, and you can see the White Cliffs of Dover on a clear day. Walking towards Calais, we come across a somewhat secluded cemetery, walled between the thorns and elders: Les Baraques. As many as a thousand soldiers from the 'Great War' are buried here. We walk subdued past long rows of stark white headstones. Reminders of fallen British, German, Australian, Canadian, South African, Indian, Egyptian, and New Zealand soldiers. The setting sun makes the '*cimetière*' even more surreal.

The world lies buried beneath this soil: so many shattered families, lonely women, and lifelong grief.

'Look at this', Nadine says softly, 'these are Chinese men, and they all died just after the war. How could that happen?' We look around silently. They appear to be workers from the Chinese Labour Corps, conscripts of the British army. According to their contract, they were not to be used as combatants. They did the heavy lifting behind the front line: mending ditches, building railways, loading and unloading ships and much more. Dirty work during ten-hour days for a daily wage of one franc. After the war, they helped clean up battlefields, exhume bodies, and clear munitions. Many of them lost their lives, while others lost their way, turning to drink or committing crimes.

Les Baraques Military Cemetery is a cemetery like the hundreds scattered in the western corner of our country, Belgium. Each grave bears witness to the machine of destruction that was the First World War, the resting place of millions of young people who had yet to well and truly begin their lives.

The First World War began in a euphoric nationalist frenzy. On railway platforms in 1914, mothers enthusiastically waved white handkerchiefs at their boys, who had barely grown out of adolescence. Fight for God and country! To Paris! To Berlin! The trite patriotism gave way to resistance and the desire for peace only after millions lost their lives. *Nie Wieder Krieg. – Never Again.* That was the lesson of the industrial meat grinder that ground up countless working and country lads.

~~~

Where trees once stood, all that is left is blackened earth. Buildings have been reduced to grey rubble; not one business is left standing. In Ukraine's city of Bakhmut, this is the horror of the conflict. Every war has its own symbol of its destructiveness. Ypres and Verdun: the First World War; Srebrenica: the civil war in the former Yugoslavia; Fallujah: the war in Iraq. Bakhmut was once an industrial city with tens of thousands of inhabitants – a proud working-class city. Now, it lies in ruins. The metallurgists of Azom lived there, along with the miners of the salt mines of Soledar and the winemakers of Artwinery. Bakhmut lived and breathed work. Men worked mainly in metalworking and salt-mining, while women were much more involved in producing wine. Artwinery was the only place in the former Soviet Union where sparkling wine was produced using the French *méthode traditionelle*. As many as fifty million bottles were stored there, ageing deep underground.

'If we're not allowed to import cava or champagne, we'll make our own', they said in Bakhmut. And so Artwinery was born, a response to the boycott against the Soviet Union at the time. We'll take care of ourselves – that's pretty much always been the spirit.

When the Nazis captured the city in late 1941, thousands of Jews were locked in the freezing cellars of a building without food or water. The residents of Bakhmut risked their lives for them: at night, they would sneak into the building and throw snowballs through the bars of the cellar door. This way, the prisoners would still have something to drink. Enraged, the Nazis walled up Jewish prisoners in one of the salt mines dotted around the town.

When you talk about miners, you're talking about resistance. In 2020, the new Zelensky government, encouraged by the International Monetary Fund and the European Union, planned to privatise the Soledar salt mines, like hundreds of other public enterprises. Never, said the people of Bakhmut. The miners demonstrated, acted, and even recorded a video message for Zelensky:

'In the past five years, eight managers have passed through here. They all had one goal: to bankrupt the company and then sell it to the private sector. We can work perfectly well without these Kyiv guests who come here twice a year and know nothing about it.'[1]

Shortly afterwards, the mines were removed from the privatisation list.

But the inhabitants of Bakhmut were no match for a sustained barrage of shells and bombs. The bombardments began in May 2022. But the real attack started in August. Exactly one year later, soldiers of Wagner's mercenary army entered the almost deserted city. Fifty thousand people reportedly lost their lives in the battle of Bakhmut. We don't know for sure because the channels of information are also contaminated in war. But what is clear is that Bakhmut had virtually no strategic importance.

Every war leaves poor buggers, workers' children, country lads or mercenaries groaning namelessly on the battlefield. This war is no different. Many Russian soldiers come from the poorer regions of the Russian Federation: the North Caucasus republics, the far eastern part of the country, and Transbaikalia. Others are men plucked from prisons and hoping for release through military service. No, there are no sons of the Russian elite here. As *Le Monde* reports, they're still holidaying in the luxury hotels of Thailand, Dubai, and the Caribbean.[2]

On the Ukrainian side, construction workers, market vendors, workers from local furniture companies, and country lads are fighting. All young recruits because the experienced soldiers are being held back for the promised great counteroffensive. *The Wall Street Journal* describes,

'The passengers were mostly poor men from villages in the

1 Oleksandr Lager and Anna Serdyuk, 'In Soledar people protest against the privatization of Artemsil', *freeradio.com.ua*, 6 March 2020.
2 Benoît Vitkine, 'The luxurious (and frowned upon) winter vacations of the Russian elite', *Le Monde*, 18 January 2023. En Ghazal Golshiri, 'A Dubaï, l'afflux des Russes provoque une flambée de l'immobilier', *Le Monde*, 24 May 2023.

north-eastern Kharkiv region, many of them unemployed, doing odd jobs as handymen or shift work at factories in the regional capital'.[3]

Trenches are crammed with youths from poor regions, partly because wealthy Ukrainians can bypass their sons' conscription by paying five thousand dollars every six months. 'The burden of sacrifice has fallen increasingly on the underprivileged', attests Luke Mogelson of *The New Yorker*. This magazine is the only one whose reporter has reached the Bakhmut front. During his twelve-day stay in the trenches around the city, Mogelson met numerous farm workers, dockworkers, plumbers, and carpenters. 'Stories abounded of Ukrainians with means of dodging conscription through graft or nepotism'.[4] Take Artem, for example, a forty-two-week-old father of three children and a clerk in a small farming community. As he'd once suffered a serious injury in a skating accident, he'd hoped it would be enough to be rejected for military service. It didn't. Artem was sent to the front line. 'I hate weapons and violence. He explains that I'm just trying to stay alive until I can get home. In his first days at the front, Artem ran away every time shells rained down. But he says he quickly learnt that running away is pointless. There is no escape from the front.[5]

US journalist Chris Hedges is familiar with these feelings and experiences. He travelled for decades for *The New York Times* from one armed conflict to another. 'I have felt the helplessness and the paralyzing fear, which, years later, descend on me like a freight train in the middle of the night, leaving me wrapped in coils of terror, my heart racing, my body dripping with sweat'.[6]

---

3 Matthew Luxmoore, '36 Hours in Bakhmut: One Unit's Desperate Battle to Hold Back the Russians', *The Wall Street Journal*, 25 May 2023.

4 Luke Mogelson, 'Two Weeks at the Front in Ukraine. In the trenches in the Donbas, infantrymen face unrelenting horrors, from missiles to grenades to helicopter fire', *The New Yorker*, 22 May 2023.

5 Ibid.

6 Chris Hedges, 'War is the greatest evil: Russia was baited into this crime –

The sobbing of people taking a fallen relative into their arms never fades away. 'War is the greatest evil', concludes the US journalist, 'War destroys all systems that sustain and nurture life – familial, economic, cultural, political, environmental, and social'.[7]

On 24 February 2022, the Russian Federation commits that greatest evil. It's the day the Russian army invades independent Ukraine on three sides, the beginning of a brutal war that kills thousands and displaces millions. Now, the battlefield is littered with corpses, and the front line is nothing but an elongated graveyard of soldiers, burnt-out tanks, and smoking wrecks of jet fighters.

but that's no excuse', *Salon*, 1 March 2022.

7 Ibid.

Vlad and Guy

Gold? Yellow, glittering, precious gold?
Much of this will make black white; foul fair;
Wrong right; base noble; old young; coward valiant;
. . . Why this?
William Shakespeare, *Timon and Athene*

In 1999, Belgian Prime Minister Guy Verhofstadt loses no time when Boris Yeltsin appoints a certain Vladimir Putin as prime minister of Russia. He rushes to Moscow to weigh up the new appointee. Putin becomes Russia's president just a few months later. In an interview with the VRT national broadcaster, Verhofstadt praises him. Putin has impressed him with 'his dossier knowledge', he is a man 'you can do business with'.[1] A remarkable friendship develops between Belgium's liberal prime minister and Russia's president. In late December 2000, Putin invites Verhofstadt to bear hunting with him, reportedly the highest honour a foreign head of government can receive. The bear hunt ultimately doesn't happen, but 'Verhofstadt was completely under the spell of Vladimir Putin', reports *De Standaard*, 'They are of the same generation and call each other "Vlad" and "Guy"'.[2]

Guy Verhofstadt is not alone. Even before Putin is sworn in as Russia's president, British Prime Minister Tony Blair and his wife Cherie head to Moscow. Liberal or Social Democrat, it makes no difference to Putin, he will roll out the red carpet for the Blairs. Tony and Cherie accompany Vladimir and Lyudmila, Putin's wife, on a visit to the tsarist summer palace just outside

1 Johan Depoortere, 'Poetin is niet gek', *DeWereldMorgen.be*, 8 April 2022.
2 *De Standaard*, 'Verhofstadt nog niet op berenjacht', 5 May 2001.

St Petersburg and the beautiful Hermitage Museum. The couples also attend the opera together at the luxurious Mariinsky theatre. [3] That same autumn, Putin is a guest in London. As bombs rain down on the Chechen capital of Grozny, Tony Blair welcomes the Russian president with the words: 'I want Russia and the West to work together to promote stability and peace'.[4]

All peace and quiet, it seems. At the same time, Blair signs arms deals with the Russian Federation until his arm hurts. Blair's close friend, US President George W. Bush, shares this view. He is lyrical about Putin: 'I looked the man in the eye. I found him to be very straightforward and trustworthy. We had a very good dialogue. I was able to get a sense of his soul; a man deeply committed to his country and the best interests of his country'.[5] Despite the dirty war in Chechnya, Putin is the good guy. This isn't about 'Vlad's' piercing blue eyes but about interests. The support is on all sides. In *The New York Times*, columnist Thomas Friedman encourages readers to 'keep rootin'' for Putin'.[6]

Everyone is lined up to give pats on the back to the former KGB agent who became president. Red carpets are in short supply for the ceremonial visits of the new Russian president in Washington, Berlin, London, and Paris. You can do business with Putin. The Kremlin's doors are banged down for arms and oil contracts. Neither the bombs raining down on the Chechen people, the banning of opposition parties in Russia, nor the clampdown on critics can dampen the fun. Chechnya is not Ukraine.

~ ~ ~

3 Ian Traynor and Michael White, 'Blair courts outrage with Putin visit', *The Guardian*, 11 March 2000.
4 Matt Kennard, 'When Tony Blair backed Putin's brutal war', *Declassified UK*, 25 March 2022.
5 C-SPAN, 'User Clip: Bush saw Putin's soul', 17 June 2021. https://www.c-span.org/video/?c4718091/user-clip-bush-putins-soul
6 Thomas L. Friedman, 'Russia's Last Line', *The New York Times*, 23 December 2001.

So, there are no dissident voices? Not exactly. In February 2000, the PTB-PVDA weekly *Solidaire* notes that Putin 'represents the new Russian bourgeoisie, the oligarchs, who want to mine the country's wealth for their own gain' and that all he has to offer are 'bombs and grenades', governing with a cocktail of 'patriotism and repression'.[7] Over in the United Kingdom, Jeremy Corbyn adopts a similar position, on which he later reflects: 'Putin was promoted into office with the support of Tony Blair and some other Western leaders. He was welcomed in the West, a state visit to Britain. At that very time, the Chechen war was going on. The appalling loss of life of Chechen people and of Russian people. The abuse of the human rights of the Chechen people, and the racism towards Chechens in Moscow and other cities were palpable. I was part of a delegation to Moscow with the parliamentary human rights group, an all-party delegation'.[8] The protests of the Belgian Marxists and the left wing of the British Labour Party fell on deaf ears. In an ironic twist of history, all those who used to knock on the doors of the Russian president's dachas are now Putin's great opponents. The Chechens had to make way for oil and gas interests. So, Putin was a great friend. But today, Putin is the devil incarnate. It's not about morality today either; it's still about interests. And those interests changed sometime before Ukraine was invaded.

---

7 Brian Becker, 'Putin offers only bombs and tanks,' Solidair, 23 February 2000, *Solidair* no. 8, p.14
8 *Double Down News*, 'Jeremy Corbyn on Putin and Ukraine', 28 February 2022.

The Russian Bear

Where money speaks
the truth falls silent.
Russian proverb

Donald Trump is a frustrated fool. Trump has a screw loose. Donald Trump is a historical blunder. When the far-right Donald Trump became president of the most powerful nation on earth, the labelling was relentless. You demonise opponents, and you do that with words. It's even more prevalent in conflicts. Putin is a lunatic. Putin is insane. It's impossible to speak to Putin. The problem with such an outlook is that it reduces all economic and political relationships to one man's psychological whims. Yet none of these amateur psychologists noticed Putin's 'lunacy' when they went to the theatre, shared a sauna, or went bear hunting with him. In fact, until 2007, the Russian president appears to have been perfectly normal.

Great minds discuss ideas; average minds discuss events; small minds discuss people, so the saying goes, and there's something to that.

Focusing only on Putin's 'deranged' character, however authoritarian he may be, obscures the contradictions and power relations of Russian society and the often-confusing conflicts in the power bloc. And they do matter, specifically, at four crucial moments: 1991, 2000, 2008, and 2014. We'll look at the watershed moment of 2014 in the next chapter.

(1) 1991

In August 1991, Boris Yeltsin announces the end of the Soviet Union from a tank. He has US President George H. W. Bush's full support. Yeltsin loses no time. He immediately sets to work on a major wave of community assets and public enterprises privatisations. Chicago School economists have come up with the formulas. After the fall of the Soviet Union, they descend on Moscow with a panel of 'experts'. These men, trained by Milton Friedman, know only one rule: *no rules, great profit.* The fact that all state institutions, from the courts to customs and social security, are collapsing is just fine with them. Only now can the free market really work, without government interference. What remains of socialism is bulldozed.

To the loud applause of the West, preventive health care, the education system, and labour rights were overhauled. Life expectancy fell dramatically, unemployment rose, and drug crime, organ trafficking and the mafia resurfaced from the depths of history. It's 'one of the greatest crimes committed against a democracy in modern history', writes Canadian journalist Naomi Klein in her bestseller *The Shock Doctrine.*[1] French economist Romaric Godin makes the same assessment: 'Russia has been traumatised by the shock therapy of the 1990s, designed to bring prosperity and keep the country among the world's major economic powers. But that has been an absolute disaster. Russia's gross domestic product collapsed along with most of the country's industrial capacity'.[2]

Anyone who thinks this all happened unopposed is sorely mistaken. By 1993, 15,000 state-owned enterprises had been sold off, but the most important sectors, gas and oil, remained

---

1 Naomi Klein, *'De shockdoctrine. De opkomst van het rampenkapitalisme'* ('The Shock Doctrine: The Rise of Disaster Capitalism'), Breda, De Geus, 2007, p.270.

2 Romaric Godin, 'Les fondements économiques de la guerre russe en Ukraine'. *Mediapart.fr*, 10 March 2022.

in government hands. Urged on by the Chicago boys, Boris Yeltsin wants to take an axe to that, too. It meets significant resistance, including in parliament. The West dismissively refers to representatives who oppose the sell-out as 'conservatives'. But to no avail: Yeltsin loses his majority in parliament. This chimes neither with the forced shock therapy nor with the president's increasingly authoritarian actions. Yeltsin raises the stakes. In September 1993, he dissolves parliament and calls new elections. But this is not the president's prerogative, and the parliament responds by deposing Yeltsin. Tens of thousands of people take to Moscow's streets to protest against forced privatisation and growing authoritarianism.

Then comes the tipping point. In the early hours of Monday, 4 October 1993, armoured vehicles break through the barricades around the Russian parliament building, the 'White House' in Moscow. As 1,300 commandos storm the White House, the artillery fire of four heavy T-80 tanks shatters the marble façade of the top floor. Yeltsin has ordered an attack on parliament. Officially, 187 people are killed and 437 wounded in the shelling of parliament, although non-governmental sources put the death toll at more than two thousand. Following the violent seizure of parliament, Yeltsin imposed an authoritarian presidential constitution through a referendum. It's still in effect today. There's no mention then of 'lunatic', 'insane', or 'deranged' in the Western narrative. Yeltsin is affectionately described as 'the flamboyant Siberian bear'.

With the road to total privatisation wide open, Yeltsin used his additional presidential powers to push through the controversial privatisation of the oil and gas sector. He launched the 'Loans for Shares' programme. The government borrowed money from wealthy financiers in return for shares in state-owned enterprises. And so, the rest of Russia's wealth was sold in the form of insider privatisation, with friendly financiers getting the tastiest bits. After a course strongly supported by the International Monetary Fund and other Western powers, this was the beginning of the oligarchs' power. In the 1996 presidential elections, Boris Yeltsin earned the oligarchs' benevolent support – their wallets.

(2) 2000

But selling out your country is not the way to run an economy. Things went downhill fast in Russia. By the summer of 1998, the country plunged into a financial crisis. Under Yeltsin, industrial production fell by more than half. It's almost inconceivable. In 1999, workers who had not been paid for years started occupying factories across the country. They disputed the legality of the privatisations. The repression was ruthless.[3] President Yeltsin's days were numbered. His domestic and foreign friends were abandoning him because chaos affects their profits. A firm hand was needed to restore order, they say. This firm hand answered to the name of Vladimir Putin. At the start of his presidency in 2000, he immediately promised to 'put Russia back on the map'. His first priority was to rein in the oligarchs who sowed chaos and poverty under Yeltsin. From then on, the Russian government began to manage the oil and gas industry itself. Gazprom acquired the private oil company Sibneft, and Rosneft took control of the private oil giant Yukos.

In October 2003, the CEO of oil giant Yukos, wealthy oligarch Mikhail Khodorkovsky, was put behind bars on suspicion of tax evasion, fraud, and embezzlement. You could put the whole oligarchy under lock and key with these accusations. But to Putin, it was a signal: the autocrats are given freedom, but the Kremlin draws the chalk lines. 'Previously the plaything of the oligarchs, the State now commands respect', says Romaric Godin. 'Mikhail Khodorkovsky's arrest was the turning point in this development'.[4]

3 'Yeltsin sneaks away', *Solidair* No. 1, 5 January 2000, p.11.
4 Romaric Godin, 'Les fondements économiques de la guerre russe en Ukraine', *Mediapart.fr*, 10 March 2022.

Putin promised stability and modernisation to the oligarchs in return. At first, he had the business cycle with him, which was leading to an economic recovery. High commodity prices boosted Russia's foreign exchange earnings from iron, nickel, aluminium, diamond, and oil and gas exports. Putin's group skilfully used this to embed several layers with various benefits and premiums in the system. Entire social groups were tied to the Kremlin through a clientelist policy.

The Russian Federation's sinewy president also had his eye on the West: he proposed to his US counterpart Bill Clinton that Russia become a member of NATO, he wanted an economic treaty with the European Union, and he offered important logistical help in George W. Bush's war on terror. Dutch journalist Monique van Ravenstein followed events closely those days. She had studied Russian and Russian affairs and worked as the coordinator of Amnesty International's Russia program. 'Since Yeltsin's drunken antics, Putin has restored Russia to a dignified international standing. Russia has joined the economic superpowers; the G7 became the G8. The instability of the 1990s and the fear of state collapse are over', she writes. 'More than anything else, 9/11 brought the United States and Russia together: the Russian and US presidents are brothers in arms against international terrorism. The European Union's criticism of Putin's policy in Chechnya has also died down.[5] Together with George W. Bush against terrorism. But the relationship was not mutual. Western institutions continued to view Russia as a defeated adversary and treated it as a toothless pawn, a regional power useful only for exporting commodities.

(3) 2008

It is starting to dawn on Putin that Russia would not be integrated into Europe or into the United States' security structures.

5 Monique van Ravenstein, 'Poetin: De Grijze Kardinaal', *Amnesty.nl*, 14 October 2002.

The Russian Federation was seen as a second-class nation, and that ate away at the Russian president. In his speech at the Munich Security Conference in February 2007, we heard a different Putin. He spoke bitterly of the West's refusal to treat Russia with respect. His outspoken criticism of the stubborn contempt of the Western powers had a clear and obvious ring to it. But no one in the West took it seriously. Nobody believed Russia could also effectively defend itself against further eastern offensives. Jack Matlock, who worked at the US Embassy in Moscow for decades and was ambassador at the time of the collapse of the Soviet Union, sums up Putin's attitude: 'Many US policies have seemed to Russians as if we're treating them as a defeated power. We're not paying attention to their national interests, we are competing with them and trying to surround them with anti-Russian states that were once part of their country'.[6]

The NATO summit in Bucharest in April 2008 marks the real break. There, in defiance of all agreements, NATO announced that both Georgia and Ukraine would become members of the military alliance. It is the third breach in a row, as the Russian Federation has twice been forced to lick the dust as NATO pushed eastwards. In two enlargement rounds – 1999 and 2004 – six countries that had been members of the Warsaw Pact, the former Soviet-led military alliance, became new NATO members. Georgia and Ukraine were next on the menu. The turning point of the Bucharest summit made Moscow realise that some will never view the Russian Federation as more than a peripheral country, destined to supply commodities to the imperial centre.

Then, the narrative also changed in the West. The good dictator, who was supplied with weapons for his dirty war against Chechnya, was recast as a bad dictator. As soon as the Russian government realised that integration with Europe and the United States is impossible, the West began to portray Putin as diabolical.

6 Octavian Report, 'From Gorbachev to Putin. An Interview with Amb. Jack Matlock', Vol. 2, No 1, 2 March 2016.

'This movie keeps replaying: Saddam Hussein of Iraq was a great hero of the US and then its villain, the same with former military leader Manuel Antonio Noriega of Panama', explains Vijay Prashad.[7]

In August 2008, Georgian troops broke the ceasefire in the Republic of South Ossetia. Russian troops respond swiftly, driving the Georgian units out of the republic. In doing so, Moscow makes it clear to everyone: this is as far as it goes and no further. The message falls on deaf ears. Meanwhile, the divisions grow within Russia. The oil-driven growth of the 2000s allowed Putin to skirt around many of these divisions. However, the 2008 economic crisis caused them to resurface. Tension was everywhere in Russia: about all the taxes that flow from the provinces to Moscow without being invested in local administrations, hospitals, education, or public transport; about the contrast between the increasingly impoverished countryside and the cities; and about the contrast between the European part of Russia and the Asian part, which was left to fend for itself. Russia topped the list of countries for wealth inequality. In fact, at that time, 36 billionaires owned as much as 60 per cent of all Russians, leading to much resentment. Protests and struggles abounded, but the trade unions and the left faced fierce repression. Popular blogger Nikolay Platoshkin, a former diplomat, became one of the most vocal critics of Putin's anti-social policies. On his YouTube channel, he incited protests against measures such as the liberal pension reforms of 2019. He was put under house arrest for five years. It was a fate shared by many trade unionists and democrats.

The wealth gap in Russia is now wider than in the United States, and that's no mean feat. In Russia, the richest 1 per cent happens to own 48 per cent of all property, while the poorest half

---

7 Vijay Prashad, 'We Do Not Want a Divided Planet; We Want a World Without Walls: The Fifteenth Newsletter (2022)', *Tricontinental.org*, 14 April 2022.

of Russians possess barely 3 per cent of the wealth.[8] Briefly put, the division of ownership in Russia is thoroughly capitalist and guarded with a heavy hand by the Russian state apparatus of Putin and his entourage.

~~~

Every era has its own peculiarities that are often lost on contemporaries, says David Criekemans, a Belgian professor of international politics. He speaks of an 'unresolved Russian question', stating that the world 'missed a golden opportunity' in the 1990s. 'After the collapse of the Soviet Union and the emergence of the independent successor states such as Russia and Ukraine, these countries could have been integrated into a global community and a strengthened international legal order based on democracy'.[9] That never happened, far from it. The attitude remains aggressive. The Cold War loser must step back and accept its role as a regional power. It has no other place than as a junior partner to the West. After 1991, Russia was stuck on the losing side of global economic developments. 'A system such as the Russian one is full of dangerous contradictions', explains Romaric Godin. 'Resolving it is complicated. It obviously involves repression, but it's also about a nationalist policy'.[10]

Given the sputtering engine at home and the growing threat from abroad, the nationalist mill was beginning to run at full speed. 'As Russians stewed in their grievance and sense of disadvantage, a gathering storm of "stab in the back" theories slowly swirled,

8 Serena Frijters, 'Russische vermogenskloof nu zelfs groter dan de Amerikaanse', *de Volkskrant*, 25 February 2022.

9 David Criekemans, 'In eine andere geopolitische Ära? Entstehen von "Eurasien" oder" Geopolitische Synthese'? Der Krieg in der Ukraine als geopolitischer Katalysator', *Welttrends*, August 2022.

10 Romaric Godin, 'Les fondements économiques de la guerre russe en Ukraine', *Mediapart.fr*, 10 March 2022.

leaving a mark on Russia's relations with the West'.[11] These are the words of William Burns. In the 1990s, he worked as an adviser at the US Embassy in Moscow. Today, he's the director of the CIA.

11 William J. Burns, *The Back Channel. A memoir of American diplomacy and the case for its renewal*, Random House Trade, p.109.

How Different it All Could Have Been

A nation that continues year after year to spend more money on military defence than on programs of social uplift is approaching spiritual doom.
     Martin Luther King, Jr.

It's Tuesday morning, 4 August 1914. The farmers in the fields around Liège are up early to bring in the harvest. At nine o'clock, when the sun is already blazing down on the fields, the farmers are flabbergasted to see a column of *uhlans* with fearsome helmets riding past their fields, followed by more soldiers on horseback. No end seems to be in sight. Then, a large group of infantrymen in grey-green uniforms and pointed helmets passes by. What is happening? The army of German general Otto von Emmich has entered Belgium, heading toward Liège. In her masterful book *De Groote Oorlog (The Great War)*, Sophie De Schaepdrijver details those first days of war:

'The German attack erupted at ten o'clock at night on 5 August during a violent thunderstorm. The machine guns of the Liège fortifications wreaked havoc on the attacking troops, whose commanders repeatedly chased them back to the fortifications in sheer rage at the failure of their plan. The air was charged with shattered, mangled, foul-smelling lead, flying back and forth and then stirring up dust. For the soldiers, who had been ordinary civilians in a previous life, it was their first confrontation with industrial death'.[1]

1 Sophie De Schaepdrijver, 'De Groote Oorlog. Het koninkrijk België tijdens de Eerste Wereldoorlog', Amsterdam, *Uitgeverij Atlas Contact*, 2013, pp. 74-75.

It takes two days for Liège to fall into German hands, giving rise to the legend of Brave Little Belgium. Antwerp falls two months later, on 10 October, and a month after that, on 22 November, the German army is finally stopped at the Yser River. From that day on, the Western Front is immersed in the static war of attrition of trench warfare, as portrayed in the book or film of the same name, *All Quiet on the Western Front*. There's nothing but news of endless death on the Western Front for four years.

After the First World War, historians and political scientists pondered whether things could have been different. How on earth had they sleepwalked into Armageddon?

The same question holds true now. On 24 February 2022, the Russian army invaded independent Ukraine on three sides. Thousands of people died, and millions fled. It's an act contrary to every international law. But again, the nagging question of whether things could have turned out differently remains. Of course, there are also events that occurred before 24 February 2022.

'The war didn't start in February last year. The war started in 2014. And since 2014, NATO allies have provided support to Ukraine, with training, with equipment, so the Ukrainian Armed Forces were much stronger in 2022, than they were in 2020, and 2014.'[2]

The speaker is not some retired military analyst. Or an ardent Putin disciple. Nobody like that at all. These are the words of NATO Secretary General Jens Stoltenberg at the NATO Summit in Brussels on 14 February 2023. Astonishingly, so little is made of what the NATO Secretary General said. But for Stoltenberg, it's clear: obviously, there was a period before the Russian invasion of

2 NATO, 'Doorstep statement by NATO Secretary General Jens Stoltenberg ahead of the meetings of NATO Defence Ministers in Brussels', 14 February 2023. https://www.nato.int/cps/en/natohq/opinions_211698.htm

Ukraine, and if you view it that way, the war has been going on for nine long years now.

Fear, ambition, and gain. For the father of historiography, the Athenian naval commander Thucydides, these are the three roots of every war. In his *History of the Peloponnesian War*, he describes the clash between the maritime empire of Athens and the heavy infantry of the Spartan Confederacy, the two dominant powers in Greece during the fifth century BC. Fear, ambition, and gain: in the current conflict, we recognise all three. The *fear* that the world's most powerful military alliance is moving closer to the borders of the Russian Federation. Russia's *ambition* is to maintain a sphere of influence within the borders of the former Soviet Union and respond to the West's condescension. The *gain* in securing economic interests, from oil exports to Ukraine's wheat seas.

Tom Sauer of the University of Antwerp explains this calmly:

'The world is a survival of the fittest between nations and superpowers. We in the European Union are no longer used to looking at geopolitics in this way, but it is still the way in which the world works. Superpowers choose to ally with smaller countries or with each other. And sometimes, they need buffer states. Just look at the world map: Ukraine is a huge country between Europe and Russia.'[3]

No one in Moscow has forgotten that the Europeans have been in Russia twice before: first, Napoleon and then the Germans in the Second World War. In no other country was the death toll of the war as high as in Russia: around 20 million. After the fall of the Berlin Wall, Russia received assurances that NATO would not move any closer to Russia, and that was the deal: Belarus and Ukraine would occupy an intermediate position as buffer states

3 Peter Casteels, 'Politoloog Tom Sauer: 'Het is perfect normaal dat Rusland Oekraïne als bufferstaat wil', *Knack.be*, 26 April 2022.

between West and East. In this spirit, the United States, Britain, and Russia signed the Budapest Memorandum in December 1994. They promised to respect 'the independence and sovereignty and the existing borders of Ukraine' and to refrain from violence, including economic violence, against the country.

~ ~ ~

The fear of which Thucydides spoke came with the Bucharest NATO summit in April 2008. It consigns all agreements to the dustbin with the decision: Ukraine and Georgia 'will join' NATO. That's when the problems over Ukraine really began, said US political scientist John Mearsheimer.

> 'According to a respected Russian journalist, Mr Putin "flew into a rage" and warned that "if Ukraine joins NATO, it will do so without Crimea and the eastern regions. It will simply fall apart".[4]

One thing is then crystal clear: Ukraine's accession to NATO would cross a deep red line.

German Chancellor Angela Merkel and French President Nicolas Sarkozy shared that view and opposed Ukraine joining NATO at the Bucharest summit. 'I was very sure that Putin would not just let that happen. That would have been a declaration of war for him', explained a confident Angela Merkel.[5] But Washington held a knife to the Europeans' throats and decided to ignore Moscow's red line. There will be a push to turn Ukraine into a NATO stronghold on the Russian border.

'Nyet Means Nyet, Russia's Nato Enlargement Redlines'. This

---

4 John Mearsheimer, 'John Mearsheimer on why the West is principally responsible for the Ukrainian crisis', *The Economist*, 19 March 2022.
5 Hans von der Burchard, 'I don't blame myself': Merkel defends legacy on Russia and Ukraine', *Politico*, 7 June 2022.

is the simple title of the telegram that the US ambassador in Moscow, William Burns, sent to Washington two months before the summit. That was on Friday, 1 February 2008. Wikileaks published the telegram. It is worth re-reading the US ambassador's warning today:

'Ukraine and Georgia's NATO aspirations not only touch a raw nerve in Russia, they engender serious concerns about the consequences for stability in the region. Not only does Russia perceive encirclement, and efforts to undermine Russia's influence in the region, but it also fears unpredictable and uncontrolled consequences which would seriously affect Russian security interests. Experts tell us that Russia is particularly worried that the strong divisions in Ukraine over NATO membership, with much of the ethnic-Russian community against membership, could lead to a major split, involving violence or, at worst, civil war. In that eventuality, Russia would have to decide whether to intervene; a decision Russia does not want to have to face.'[6]

In other words, Washington is well aware of what an eastward enlargement of NATO would mean.

6 Wikileaks, 'Nyet Means Nyet: Russia's NATO Enlargment Redlines', 1 February 2008.
https://wikileaks.org/plusd/cables/08MOSCOW265_a.html

The Maidan

US diplomat Jack Matlock said,

'NATO commanders are talking about Russia as an existential threat. But we're even more of an existential threat to them', 'Unlike them, we are fiddling around, trying to control governments even militarily that were once part of their territory. They look at us much more seriously as an existential threat than we conceivably could look at them'.

Matlock was not proclaiming a minority position.

'Almost every one of us in senior positions in both parties that helped negotiate the end of the Cold War opposed the expansion of NATO to the east. It wasn't that we didn't want to protect Eastern Europe. We said, "Use a different mechanism," whether we were Republicans or Democrats.'[1]

The other mechanism that was supposed to ensure peace and stability in Eastern Europe never materialised. Basking in the glow of the new unipolar world led by the United States, Washington's hawks and neocons pushed through NATO enlargement. Despite and contrary to the Budapest Memorandum. Pressure was exerted from the European side to integrate Ukraine into the structures of the European Union. Negotiations on a free trade agreement (FTA) between the European Union and Ukraine stalled at the end of November 2013. The proposed FTA was tied to a $17 billion

1 Octavian Report, 'From Gorbachev to Putin. An Interview with Amb. Jack Matlock', Vol. 2, No 1, 2 March 2016.

loan from the International Monetary Fund. Added conditions included raising the retirement age for women, cutting corporate taxes, 'reforming' public water and energy supplies, and phasing out several 'bothersome' labour and environmental regulations. While President Viktor Yanukovych was not opposed to an agreement with the European Union as such, he wanted to leave the door open to Moscow as well. He did not sign the agreement. Moscow played it cleverly. It offered a $15 billion Russian aid package with a 33 per cent discount on Russian natural gas. 'During 2010-2013, Yanukovych pushed neutrality', explains US economics professor Jeffrey Sachs. Sachs is no idle voice; this man has advised three UN secretaries-general and knows a thing or two about international politics. Sachs claims that after the FTA was cancelled, the US began working covertly to overthrow Yanukovych.[2]

The narrative turned Yanukovych into a pro-Russian president. Anyone not in favour of joining the European Union had to be pro-Moscow. It was campism: if you're not with us, you're against us. Even so, Yanukovych meekly implemented the privatisation demanded by the International Monetary Fund. He also faced significant opposition in Ukraine. A mix of socio-economic discontent and pro-Western sentiment brought thousands of people to Kyiv's independence square, the Maidan, on 21 November 2013. At once, they received the full support of the West and all manner of NGOs working on the recipe for successful colour revolutions. The conflict played out and gradually became violent. Among others, US Deputy Secretary of State Victoria Nuland and the leader of the liberal group in the European Parliament, Guy Verhofstadt, travelled to Maidan to lend their support to the protests against the incumbent president.

With Cargill and its ilk laughing all the way to the bank in the wings, they wanted Ukraine to sign new free trade agreements with Europe and the United States. They also wanted to get rid of

2 Jeffrey D. Sachs, 'The War in Ukraine Was Provoked—and Why That Matters to Achieve Peace', *Commondreams.org*, 29 May 2023.

the elected president, Yanukovych. For the record, such conduct is more than a diplomatic breach. Imagine if, during the protests against French President Macron's pension reform, a US State Department official descended on Paris to call for the president's removal. The fact that right-wing extremists were openly active in the square did not seem to matter. Idesbald Goddeeris, a professor of history at KULeuven, said on the radio at the time: 'Europe has added fuel to the fire, partly through the actions of Guy Verhofstadt. In the European Parliament, he took a sharp stance against fascists. Now, he's going to cheer them on in Kyiv. Europe will come to regret this. We've become a party to it. There's no end in sight yet.'[3]

Yanukovych was overthrown on 22 February 2014. The chairman of parliament, Oleksandr Turchynov, was appointed interim president. Weeks of anti-Maidan protests began in eastern Ukraine, culminating in the occupation of administrative buildings in Kharkiv, Donetsk, and Lugansk. Thousands of people continued to guard the occupied buildings at night, while the central squares of the city filled up during the day. The protesters rejected the Maidan in Kyiv along with the economic and political discrimination of the Donbas industrial basin. Interim President Turchynov did not engage with the protest movement. Instead, he ordered a 'counter-terrorism operation': the military had to break the resistance. With growing extremism on both sides, it was the beginning of a bloody civil war. One that would take the lives of 14,000 people by 2022.

Jens Stoltenberg is right: the war started in 2014. If the European Union and the United States had accepted the 2014 protests in the East as legitimate expressions, there would have been no counter-terrorism operation and no civil war. Not a single Western voice called for adequate political representation for the southeast or warned against the escalation of the conflict. Perhaps such a voice

3 Dominique Fiers, 'Interventie Verhofstadt pervers of dom', *VRT NWS*, 22 February 2014.

would have been enough to halt the cycle of violence. Those who want a living democracy in Ukraine must consider all the country's population groups, both in the west and the southeast.

~~~

Fortunately, the Minsk agreements were reached in 2014 and 2015 under the supervision of the Organisation for Security and Co-operation in Europe, signed by Ukraine, Russia, France, and Germany. The agreements link a ceasefire to federal state reform, with a separate status for Russian-speaking regions inside Ukraine as a whole. Not unlike the Belgian model. But the Minsk agreements remained a dead letter. That seemed to be the intention. The ceasefire was constantly broken, and there was no sign of state reform. The West's main aim with the agreements was to buy time to equip Ukraine militarily and ideologically against Russia. In 2022, when German Chancellor Angela Merkel felt vindicated by the Russian invasion, she openly admitted as much. 'Ukraine has also used this time to become stronger, as we can see today', she told *Die Zeit*.[4] Professor Jeffrey Sachs concurs:

'After Yanukovych's overthrow, the war broke out in the Donbas, while Russia claimed Crimea. The new Ukrainian government appealed for NATO membership, and the US armed and helped restructure the Ukrainian army to make it interoperable with NATO. In 2021, NATO and the Biden Administration strongly recommitted to Ukraine's future in NATO.'[5]

Washington then does its utmost to train and equip the

4 Tina Hildebrandt and Giovanni di Lorenzo, 'Angela Merkel: 'Hatten Sie gedacht, ich komme mit Pferdeschwanz?'', *Zeit.de*, 7 December 2022.
5 Jeffrey D. Sachs, 'The War in Ukraine Was Provoked—and Why That Matters to Achieve Peace', *Commondreams.org*, 29 May 2023.

Ukrainian army, including inviting Ukrainian forces to participate in NATO military exercises. Moscow, fearing that Ukraine would become a *de facto* member of the alliance, sent President Biden a letter on 17 December 2021, requesting written guarantees that Ukraine would remain outside the alliance and observe strict neutrality. A month later, on 26 January 2022, Secretary of State Antony Blinken replied dryly, 'There is no change; there will be no change'.[6] One month on, Russia attacked Ukraine.

Political scientist John Mearsheimer, explains:

'The Monroe Doctrine, established by the United States in the nineteenth century, seems to have inspired the Russian position on this issue. The doctrine stipulated that no major power should station military troops in the States' backyard.

'With diplomacy failing to resolve what Russians see as an existential problem, their president has unleashed a war'.[7]

That said, the Russian invasion is a gross violation of the United Nations Charter and an act of aggression under international law. The attack also violated Russian guarantees to Ukraine in the 1994 Budapest Memorandum, when Russia promised to respect Ukraine's sovereignty and borders in exchange for Kyiv giving up its nuclear weapons.

~ ~ ~

Vladimir Putin reaches for the worn-out toolbox of nationalism to justify one and all. Days before invading, he tries to tell the world that Ukraine is not a nation, but an artificially separated part of the Russian nation. In this speech, the Russian president hits out at Lenin, who recognised Ukraine's right to self-

---

6 John Mearsheimer, 'Pourquoi les grandes puissances se font la guerre', *Le Monde Diplomatique*, August 2023, pp.10-11.
7 Ibid.

determination after the Russian Revolution of 1917. To Putin, this was a historic blunder, and Ukraine is nothing more than an artificial state. With this deeply ahistorical argument, he tries to crush relations between the Russian and Ukrainian peoples under the hammer of chauvinism. It's the return of the Great Russian ideology of the Tsarist era, when – in Lenin's words – people were held in the prison of Great Russian chauvinism.

The war in Ukraine has revived the spectre of nationalism. Unity against the enemy! Nationalism always relies on inclusion and exclusion as its template for social order. Inclusion of the good, exclusion of the bad. It uses history, culture, ethnicity, and religion to build walls and create ill-fated feuds.[8]

Nationalism is back in Europe. It rages in all its ugliness in the East. In Ukraine, Great Russian chauvinism is met with ethnic nationalism. Far-right groups are fanning the flames. They make no secret of their admiration for the Nazi collaborators of the Second World War. Aryan, Christian and blue-eyed they describe themselves as the true descendants of the chosen master race, the *Herrenvolk*. This opened the floodgates.

8 Werner Ruf, *Zeitenwende?* Zeitschrift Marxistische Erneuerung nr. 130, June 2022, p.62

The Year 1962

When the rich go to war, it's the poor who die.
  Jean-Paul Sartre

A few months before the Russian invasion, high-level talks were held at the Pentagon. A *Washington Post* journalist, David Ignatius, turned the talks into world news. Its contents can be summed up as follows: Sending US troops to Ukraine is out of the question. After all, President Biden has just decided to withdraw his troops from Afghanistan to focus on arch-rival China. But perhaps the key lies somewhere in the Afghan experience? The US Army took a beating there and had to leave with its tail between its legs. What if we did what the Afghans did to us? A long war to exhaust the Russian army and regime, constantly fed with an endless stream of weapons. David Ignatius writes,

> 'It's an ironic example of turning the tables, weighing whether and how to inflict harm similar to what US forces have suffered in recent years'.[1]

The plan receives broad support. Two major think tanks, the Council on Foreign Relations and the Atlantic Council, echo this line of reasoning and keep the public informed with emphatic references to 'the Afghan trap'.

In 1978, the United States and its allies began to fund far-right-wing forces in Afghanistan who fashioned themselves as the *mujahedin*. They conducted attacks against the communist-

---

1 David Ignatius, 'Opinion. The Biden administration weighs backing Ukraine insurgents if Russia invades', *The Washington Post,* 19 December 2021.

led government. To defend that government, the USSR entered Afghanistan in 1979. The US then decided to increase its support of the *mujahedin*, working with its allies (such as Saudi Arabia and Pakistan) to inflame a 'religious war'. The war would drag on for a decade, resulting in an estimated 1.8 million civilian casualties. Russian troop losses and the economic cost of the war helped trigger the collapse of the Soviet Union. The foreign fighters who sided with the *mujahideen* would later become al-Qaeda's foot soldiers. It's not exactly an experiment worth repeating, or so you'd think. But Washington thinks otherwise. Hillary Clinton does not hide her enthusiasm while explaining the strategy to the news channel MSNBC.

'Remember, the Russians invaded Afghanistan. Although no country went in, they certainly had a lot of countries supplying arms and advice, and even some advisers to those who were recruited to fight Russia. It didn't end well for the Russians. A very motivated and then funded and armed insurgency basically drove the Russians out of Afghanistan. I think that is the model that people are looking toward.'[2]

This is the option that does the trick. No attempts to prevent the war with negotiations. But also, no US boots on the ground.

Luck never runs out for the big arms manufacturers. Late January 2022, Greg Hayes, the CEO of Raytheon Technologies, addressed his shareholders to announce good news, one month before the invasion of Ukraine. 'We are seeing opportunities for international sales', he explains. 'The tensions in Eastern Europe, the tensions in the South China Sea, all of those things are putting pressure on some of the defence spending over there. So, I fully expect we're going to see some benefit from it'.[3] War is always bad

2 Hillary Clinton, on MSNBC, 1 March 2022.
3 The Motley Fool, 'Raytheon Technologies (RTX) Q4 2021 Earnings Call Transcript', 25 January 2022.

for people and good for the arms industry. Because they benefit. The United States is emptying its stockpiles and sending $21 billion worth of missiles and anti-aircraft artillery to Ukraine. One and a half million projectiles are sent there for the howitzers alone. Each one costs $800. As these reserves need to be replenished, the weapons factories are running at full capacity.

Uppsala University in Sweden keeps accurate records of all the wars between 1946 and 2021.[4] And there's a lot of them. Researchers at the Centre for Strategic and International Studies delve into the dataset to analyse the data. The findings of that research sound logical: either a war ends relatively quickly, or it drags on. A quarter of all wars end in less than a month. Another quarter lasts less than a year. However, researchers say that wars that last longer than a year tend to last a decade on average. That happens because both sides dig in their heels. Then it becomes a war of positions, fought for years over a few square miles of no-man's land.[5] Protracted wars rarely end with one side winning. When neither side is strong enough to crush the other, wars still end in some sort of peace agreement. 'That means fighting is going to continue. It's going to be bloody. It's going to be hard. And at some point, both sides will either negotiate a settlement, or it will come to a military conclusion at some point in the future', US Joint Chiefs of Staff Chairman General Mark Milley said straight-faced in May 2023 about the war in Ukraine.[6]

The irony is that it is not even Russia that will find it hardest to refrain from a protracted war of position. Despite the sanctions, the Russian economy is doing better than expected. Ukrainians

4 UCDP/PRIO Armed Conflict Dataset version 23.1 https://ucdp.uu.se/downloads/index.html#armedconflict
5 Center for Strategic and International Studies, How Does It End? What Past Wars Tell Us about How to Save Ukraine. *Csis.org*, 4 March 2022.
6 U.S. Department of Defense, 'Secretary of Defense Lloyd J. Austin III and Joint Chiefs of Staff Chairman General Mark A. Milley Hold a News Conference Following a Virtual Meeting of the Ukraine Defense Contact Group', 25 May 2023.

are the main victims. Anxious families, sons not returning from the front, missing children, but also an infrastructure that is being destroyed day by day, businesses shuttered as workers fight at the front, and ports closed. Every day of a lengthened war is an additional day of suffering.

'An unwinnable war', is how the Rand Corporation describes it in the magazine *Foreign Affairs*.[7] Rand, the US military think-tank with more than 1,800 employees, wonders aloud whether the United States has any idea what the endgame of this war is. Chas Freeman, who spent a lifetime in the Foreign Service, including a stint as ambassador to Saudi Arabia, sums up the mood in Washington,

> 'There seems to be a lot of people in the United States who think that's just dandy: it's good for the military-industrial complex; it reaffirms our negative views of Russia; it reinvigorates NATO; it puts China on the spot. What's so terrible about a long war? If you're not Ukrainian, you probably see some merit in a long war.'[8]

The Ukrainian people deserve to live in peace, with borders respected and without the constant threat of renewed violence from Russia. The question is how to achieve that.

Fidel Castro and his *barbudos* toppled the Cuban dictator, Fulgencio Batista, on New Year's Eve 1958. Cuba no longer wants to be a neo-colony of the United States and demands its sovereignty. Washington takes a dim view of this and immediately forges plans to overthrow Castro. The US sent a mercenary army to the Cuban Bay of Pigs in April 1961. The enemy attack is repulsed.

7 Samuel Charap, 'An Unwinnable War. Washington Needs an Endgame in Ukraine', *Foreign Affairs*, 5 June 2023.
8 Aaron Maté, 'US fighting Russia "to the last Ukrainian": veteran US diplomat', *The Grayzone*, 24 March 2022.

After the failed invasion, the Cubans turned to the Soviet Union for military defence. But Moscow has its own agenda. The United States has just deployed intermediate-range missiles in Turkey and Italy aimed at the Soviet Union. Washington began testing nuclear weapons again in April 1962. Moscow deployed nuclear missiles in Cuba in May of that year, which American U-2 reconnaissance aircraft discovered in August. The Cuban Missile Crisis is a fact.

The world teetered on the brink of nuclear war between the United States and the Soviet Union. Cuba was just the *lieu de spectacle*, the place where it happened. Neither superpower accepted nuclear weapons in their backyards. And today is no different, really: Moscow does not accept that Ukraine is part of the nuclear-armed NATO empire. Yet war was avoided in 1962. This was a victory of diplomacy, not of force. The Soviet Union withdrew its nuclear weapons. Shortly afterwards, the US dismantled its intermediate-range missiles in northern Italy and Turkey. There were no contracts or other arrangements, no paper. A handshake, at most. But it worked. Cuba was not even part of the deal. The superpowers arranged it between themselves. Anyone looking for a solution to the bloody war in Ukraine today should remember 1962.

Perhaps Mike Mullen, the former US Army Chief of Staff, is calling for negotiations with 1962 in mind. 'We need to do everything we possibly can to try to get to the table to resolve this thing. As is typical in any war, it has got to end, and usually, there are negotiations associated with that. The sooner, the better, as far as I'm concerned.'[9] Negotiating does not mean conceding victory to Russia but ending the escalating violence as soon as possible and seeking a lasting diplomatic solution attractive enough for both countries to lay down their arms. It's the only way. Ultimately, European security also depends on how this conflict ends. Of

9 *ABC News*, 'This Week' Transcript 10-9-22: White House NSC Coordinator for Strategic Communications John Kirby & Adm. Mike Mullen', 9 October 2022.

course, negotiations can be lengthy. More than five hundred sessions were required for the talks that suspended the Korean War in the 1950s. A ceasefire and demilitarized zones could be a start. One thing is certain: Ukraine's future security and development must be front and centre in the talks.

Chapter 6

The Voices
Below Deck

The Captains and the Lower Deck

Another world is not only possible, she is on her way. Maybe many of us won't be here to greet her, but on a quiet day, if I listen very carefully, I can hear her breathing.
Arundhati Roy

As the old saying goes, fish discover water last. Likewise, living in an ocean of experiences and stories, we struggle to make sense of our world.

But for Tim Gurner, it's all pretty simple. He runs the Australian Gurner Group, a property firm that specialises in luxury homes for the better-off among us. The group has a portfolio of €5.7 billion. With a personal fortune of €562 million, Gurner is also not short of cash himself. Speaking at the Australian Financial Review Property Summit in early September 2023, Gurner spends barely a minute explaining exactly how the world works and what we need to do to make it work better:

'The problem is that people decided that they didn't really want to work so much anymore through COVID, and that has had a massive issue on productivity. You know, tradies have definitely pulled back on productivity. You know, they have been paid a lot to do not too much in the last few years. And we need to see that change. We need to see unemployment rise. Unemployment has to jump 40, 50 per cent, in my view. We need to see the pain in the economy. We need to remind people that they work for the employer, not the other way around. I mean, there's been a systematic change where employees feel the employer is extremely lucky to have them as opposed to the other way around. So, it's a dynamic that has to change. We've got to kill that attitude, and that has to come through hurting the economy, which is what the whole world is trying to do. The governments around the world are trying to increase unemployment to get back to some sort of normality. And we're seeing, I think every employer now is seeing it. I mean, there is definitely massive layoffs going off. People might not be talking about it, but people are definitely laying people off. And we're starting to see less arrogance in the employment market. And that has to continue because that will cascade across the cost balance.'[1]

People who are so brutally honest are rare. I think we owe Tim Gurner a debt of gratitude for the whole humanity-and-world-view sandwich he's serving up here.

When Gurner talks about people 'who have been paid a lot to do not too much in the last few years', he's not talking about property tycoons like himself, who have become filthy rich in recent years through the massive injection of money, not into activities relating to real needs, but into investments and property. The people whom the Australian multimillionaire despises are working people, the 'tradies'. Those who did the dirty work in the pandemic and then got the faltering engine of recovery going. And who are already forgotten today, in a world where rampant inflation is eroding their savings.

Interestingly, Gurner refers to the Covid period, precisely when the working class was able to find a new sense of pride. We're the indispensable ones, the ones who keep things going, and we're no longer satisfied with some applause from the balcony. That was the subject of my previous book, *They Have Forgotten Us*.

Working-class pride is also evident in the new wave of

1 Financial Review [@FinancialReview], 'Gurner Group founder Tim Gurner tells the Financial Review Property Summit workers have become "arrogant" since COVID and "We've got to kill that attitude", *X.com*, 12 September 2023.

industrial action in the United States today. Todd Vachon is the trade union expert at Rutgers University in New Jersey. He explains the new wave as follows:

'During the pandemic, you saw many workers who didn't have a union but organised collectively to enforce safe working conditions. Many realised that their wishes would be granted if they represented them collectively'.[2]

But Gurner wants to eliminate this burgeoning awareness; in his words, 'We've got to kill that attitude'. Gurner's speech places him in the long stream of elitism that has emerged from neoliberalism.

Author Ayn Rand was one of the stars of the glory years of Margaret Thatcher and Ronald Reagan. Her bestseller *Atlas Shrugged* tells us that 'workers and other mediocre people' are parasites on the genius and effort of the gifted few. By imposing all sorts of regulations, governments and stupid citizens are just putting spokes in smart entrepreneurs' wheels. The elite, not the working class, create wealth. And it is high time the world was rebuilt on 'the virtue of greed'.[3] That kind of mentality.

~~~

According to Gurner, we need to 'hurt the economy' and increase unemployment by half to return to 'normality'. By 'hurt', the property tycoon doesn't have himself in mind. The hurt is for others, not for the financial vultures who demand 15 per cent returns on production. For Gurner, the fruits of labour should not go to people through decent wages, but to bloated dividends.

2 Roeland Termote, 'In Amerika vinden de vakbonden hun tweede adem'. *De Standaard*, 9 September 2023.
3 Cited in Corey Robin, *The reactionary mind. Conservatism from Edmund Burke to Sarah Palin*, Oxford University Press, New York, 2011, p.90.

Naturally, he is silent on fair taxation, which would tax property groups like his so governments could invest more in education, health, public transport and environmental transition. The hurt he proposes would leave hundreds of thousands of families destitute, pushing them out of the economy and marginalising them. Although it sounds borderline insane, it's no different to the recession therapy of Margaret Thatcher and Ronald Reagan in the early 1980s. That's what the second chapter of this book covered. Multimillionaires like Gurner want to relive it all over again, back to the future in a flawed time machine.

'Arrogant', is how Gurner describes people who strive for a well-paid job to live a decent life. Mass redundancies are his prescription. It fits into a view of the world in which people are things, disposable products, and replaceable things like Kleenex tissues. Gurner wants to 'change the dynamic of society', not towards more solidarity and collectivity, but towards everyone for themselves in a war of all against all. To his mind, that is the 'normal' order of things. This echoes Margaret Thatcher's words when she wanted to eliminate 'the heart and soul of the nation', with any sense of belonging.

The truth finally comes out at the end of Gurner's speech: 'And that has to continue because that will cascade across the cost balance'. What cost balance? Those of destitute families? Or of crumbling working-class neighbourhoods of the British Midlands and the American Rust Belt? Or of the society that must pay for all this misery? No, it's about the cost balance of his property empire. His love goes not through his stomach but through his wallet.

It's no coincidence that Gurner likes to introduce himself as a captain of industry. In fact, it's the term used by someone who views the whole of society as a military event, with captains in command of an obedient army of foot soldiers. In his one-minute speech, he uses the word 'need' seven times. Just as in feudal society when the apprentice had to be unquestioningly loyal to his master, the serf to his lord of the manor, society to the king and the king to God, so

Gurner demands loyalty from working people. The businessman as a born military man to whom one owes absolute obedience.

~~~

You can also detect a hint of panic in all of Gurner's 'needs'. You get that a lot: people who hide their insecurity behind tough words. Fear of a different world where the people who produce the wealth are also at the helm of society. The captain's fear of the people below deck, where sweating, toiling, working, drinking, and cursing are the order of the day. Fear of the nurse Kath engaging in her first social action, fear of the trade unionist Harsev organising the Indian workers' community in London, and fear of the Beirut grocer Bazazo, who is weary of the dollar determining his life.

Kath, Harsev, Bazazo, Emma, Jean, Tim, and Liam are all featured in this book, and what strikes me is how often the same words are repeated. They echo through the ship's hold: safety, respect, pride, sovereignty, connection, peace, commitment, and hope. In our world, with its quays full of goods and languages, human sighs are strikingly universal. On Twitter, the channel now known as X, Elon Musk's private playpen, 20 million people respond to Gurner's statements. Responses come in from all corners of the planet. From everywhere, they step into the breach of the world of labour.

Our world has oceans of commitment. People are involved in their neighbourhoods, at work, in things close to their hearts. This commitment often remains in the dark, especially if it is collective. Collective struggle is the building block of change. Without commitment, there is no action; without action, there is no awareness, and without awareness and action, there is no change. This is what makes the powers that be respond. It has never been any other way. Any movement that tried to break the status quo towards social progress, freedom and justice was pilloried and repressed. From the Thracian gladiator Spartacus and his army of freed slaves to peasant leaders such as Zeger Janssone, who led one of the largest peasant uprisings in Europe in 1325 and, for his efforts, was tortured on a wheel, beheaded and hanged from the highest gallows in Bruges. From Till Eulenspiegel and the Beggars in the Spanish kingdom to the radical enlighteners of Paris and Port-au-Prince. From the first industrial actions in Manchester and the Borinage to Patrice Lumumba's and Thomas Sankara's struggles in Africa. Resistance meets opposition.

And today is no different. A man like Jeremy Corbyn is the target of slander and lies. Climate action and union struggles are criminalised. Parties are branded as 'populist' and 'extremist' or worse. This narrative can only be deciphered in one way: as a sign of weakness, as the ugly convulsions of a world in decline. People want the simple things in life: a decent income, a healthy meal, a roof over their heads and affordable energy. They come together, organise, and stand up. As long as there is oppression and injustice, there will be resistance.

Meanwhile, we live in a polarised world that can tilt either way. The demons are never far away. Hope is a verb; you must keep building on it. By helping people stand up, speak out and unite. Through education and action. By taking a stance on what is right in this world And uniting these movements in the search for a new socialism, a society without plunder, hatred, and oppression, which respects the sources of its wealth: labour and nature.

Mutiny as a Metaphor

I am no longer accepting the things I cannot change.
I am changing the things I cannot accept.
    Angela Davis

January 2023. The waves crash roughly against the Malecon quay. We stroll among young couples on Havana's seaside boulevard. Belkys tells me that she wrote her Master's dissertation on Charles V and the Spanish Empire in Cuba.

Belkys captures my attention immediately. Charles was the son of Philip the Handsome and Joanna of Castile, better known as Joanna the Mad. When the little man let out his newborn cry in Ghent's Prinsenhof on 24 February 1500, no one could have predicted that he would grow up to become the great Emperor Charles. Wealth is hereditary, and Charles was a wealthy man. Over the years, he came to own the Habsburg principalities in Central Europe, Milan, Franche-Comté and the Netherlands through his paternal grandparents. On his mother's side, he inherited Castile, Aragon, Navarre, Naples, Sicily, Sardinia, the Canary Islands, Hispaniola, Cuba, and the pearl coast of Venezuela. In the first years of his reign as King of Castile and Aragon, Spanish conquistadores still conquered the vast Aztec and Inca empires. This continued until Charles V ruled over an empire stretching across the four continents. It was the first empire of its kind.

In 1512, Cuba also came under Spanish control, and the island immediately took on a special status, Belkys explained. For three centuries, Havana was the Spanish Empire's port across the ocean. From there, virtually all the gold and silver plundered from Latin America was shipped to European motherland. *Open Veins of Latin*

239

America is how Uruguayan writer Eduardo Galeano described this exploitation in his brilliant classic of the same name. Belkys tells me that the Spanish did not build a city as majestic as Havana anywhere in the Caribbean or Latin America. As she tells her story, I see the old colonial splendour behind the new licks of paint. 'That might bind us', I say, 'because that great empire also ruled the Low Countries then'. In the Spanish Empire, the Seventeen Provinces, as our regions were called, were the economic hub. Our regions participated in the first globalisation from the outset. Cities and businesses were established using the looted wealth. At the time, international trade in the Netherlands was through Antwerp. It became the distribution centre of choice: from Canarian sugar to all kinds of spices. Old warehouses, through which tobacco and sugar from Cuba passed, are still tucked away here and there in the city. Havana and Antwerp, two hubs, two ports, at opposite ends of the Spanish route.

I also tell Belkys about the resistance in our Low Countries to Spanish rule, from nobles yearning for autonomy to innkeepers, vagabonds, and penniless peasants. *'Ce ne sont que des gueux'*, they are but beggars, the Spanish governess Margaret of Parma would disparagingly call them. The name 'beggars' spreads quickly as a badge of honour among all those who wanted to escape the Spanish yoke. 'Then we're all beggars', Belkys laughs.

Since then, we have recognised the word in Dutch as a 'sobriquet'. A sobriquet is a nickname or byname used as a title of honour. Perhaps we should do the same with the word 'mutiny'. I heard the term from Fiona Hill, the former National Security Council staffer in the United States. She speaks aghast of 'mutiny' by the countries of the Global South no longer following Washington's wishes. 'Mutiny' is a sobriquet, but it is also a metaphor, an implied comparison, and an image of disobeying the ruling order.

~~~

From the empire of Charles to the ancient Silk Roads, our world is always inextricably linked. And the sea plays a part in that story. Somewhere in the landlubbers among us – and that's almost all of us – there is an unconscious assumption that history is only made on land. It was as if the oceans were anti-spaces, empty interspaces between land masses. That has never been the case. What would the empires of the Persians and the Greeks, the Romans and the Ottomans, the Venetians and the Chinese, the Dutch and the British have been without the sea? The transport of wealth, colonial troops and enslaved people would not have been possible without the oceans that colour our planet blue. Water was the trade route. And it was not all calm on the water, quite the contrary.

The naval fleets of the eighteenth century were imposing sites of social hierarchy and labour exploitation. For twenty-four hours a day, hundreds, sometimes almost a thousand sailors had to work there, under dangerous conditions, in great ethnic and national diversity, and subject to the almost unlimited power of the ship's officers. Cruel punishments, from flogging to execution, awaited those who stirred up trouble. Navy vessels were the factories of the sea, and resistance was more common than not. One in ten slave ships experienced a mutiny. In the colonial eighteenth century, as many as one in three merchant ships mutinied. Historians who have recently studied the turbulent history of maritime resistance note that mutiny is a broad concept that encompasses all forms of collective resistance. From singing together below deck to petitions and refusing to work to sabotage and take over the ship.[1] For example, I had never heard of the round robin, a common means of protest among sailors who wanted to air their grievances.

1 Niklas Frykman, Clare Anderson, Lex Heerma van Voss and Marcus Rediker. *Mutiny and Maritime Radicalism in the Age of Revolution: An Introduction*. International Review of Social History, Volume 58, Special Issue S21: Mutiny and Maritime Radicalism in the Age of Revolution: A Global Survey, 2013, pp.1-14. Published online by Cambridge University Press, 6 September 2013.

They would draw a circle and write their demands in it. They wrote their names around the circle to conceal who had started the petition and avoid individual beatings. The more names, the greater the power in the expanding circle. 'One and all' was the favourite slogan in this respect.

Ships carried not only goods, war, and enslaved people. They also carried ideas, both below and above the deck. News, rumours, information, and insights flowed across the Atlantic along the swelling arteries of trade that linked Nantes and Bordeaux with Cape Haitien, Port-au-Prince, Havana and Kingston. These trade routes brought countless ships and seafarers to all kinds of ports, together with refugees and veterans of battle. On these journeys across the ocean and through the Caribbean, the rebels in Jamaica and Santo Domingo gained new insights into the political developments occurring in London and Paris. In the world of trade and slave plantations, the sea, not the land, was the network of communication. The ideas of collectivism and egalitarianism moved from revolutionary France to Santo Domingo and then to Jamaica, Cuba and back again through this global water network, the www of the day. The visions of the Jacobin republic in France inspired the uprisings in Haiti and Santo Domingo, and vice versa.

Mutiny is a metaphor for the great spirit of freedom that has travelled the oceans from the outset and enriched itself in the process. All those years, from Emperor Charles to the present day, have shown how closely the mutinies of the North and South have been intertwined for five centuries. Today is no different, no matter how many walls we build in our minds and between continents. They call it a mutiny when workers and employees unite to fight for decent wages and working conditions or when social action rallies for democratic rights or for our climate. They call it a mutiny when countries and peoples want to decide for themselves what to do with their resources, whether lithium or cobalt and claim the right to process their resources. They call it a mutiny when countries and peoples refuse to take sides in a trade war and a new cold war imposed on them by Washington. They call it a mutiny that the unipolar era of the United States is quietly coming to an end. As this mutiny is on the right wave of history, let's embrace it.

Harsev recalls that in India, we saw the largest social action in human history, when farmers and workers mobilised together. In Latin America, popular movements from Bolivia to Chile bring about democratic reform. They represent hope.

Mutiny is also stirring in the north. The class struggle ebbs and flows like the waves of the sea. But it exists, and it fights against the same world order, the same monopolies, the same system of exploitation.

In March 2023, more than three million people took to the streets in France to demand decent pensions and to keep the retirement age at sixty-two. The movement lasted throughout the first half of the year, including fourteen national days of action. Remarkable numbers of young people, students and pupils participated. Not since 1968 have so many people taken to the streets in France. That's a deep commitment. The United Kingdom has seen more social action in recent years than in the turbulent 1970s. In Spain and Belgium, there has been no end to actions and demonstrations for wage increases and pensions since the end of the pandemic. Wage disputes are also on the rise in Germany, among garbage collectors and metal workers at Lufthansa and in healthcare.

A new generation of activists is emerging in the United States. Newspapers describe them as 'young and pro-union'. They include young unionist Nabretta Hardin, who started the union at Starbucks, and the charismatic Chris Smalls, who did the same at Amazon. In the summer of 2023, Hollywood scriptwriters and then actors went on strike. The 150,000 workers at Ford, General Motors, and Stellantis in Detroit conducted targeted strikes in 2023 over pay rises and the restoration of their eroded pension plans. For the third summer in a row, US media are talking about 'the summer of strikes'. More than 70 per cent of Americans expressed support for unions in 2022, the highest level since 1965.

I know: the struggle is fragile; it rises and falls. But the idea that there would be neither collective action nor resistance in the north of our planet is utter nonsense. If we can get the mutiny of the North to lend a hand to the mutiny of the South, and vice versa, we can tilt the world in the democratic, social and ecological direction this planet needs.